# Praise for *Thrift*

"'Where materialism thrives thrift hides' - not so, of course: they need one another. Spending and saving, like virtue and wisdom, are matters of the soul as much as the ledger. This book by the ever erudite Dr. Malloch provides a timely reminder from someone who knows a lot about both money and virtue, that there is more to life and money than credit or cash."

> **—Very Rev. Dr. Christopher Hancock,**
> King's College, London University

"Thrift is not avarice. Avarice is not generous. Historically, it is the thrifty people who are generous. If we want a society of true wealth, a giving society, we will need to rediscover the virtue of thrift so well expounded in this book that should become a true classic."

> **— Paul Dietrich**, CEO, Foxhall Capital

"According to the ever-wise Dr. Samuel Johnson, 'Frugality may be termed the daughter of Prudence, the sister of Temperance, and the parent of Liberty.' This book is most noteworthy because it puts us back on such a virtuous path!"

> **—Jim Stanley,** Co-Chairman, VII, Inc.

"Edison like all inventors knew that the scope of thrift is limitless. So did Dr. Land the founder of Polaroid, one of our companies. Ted Malloch has done all of us in business a huge favor—he has rediscovered a virtue that unlocks the door to success and builds true character."

> **— Mary Jeffries**, CEO, Polaroid

*(Continued)*

"This is a most interesting and timely topic—not exactly politically correct nor the kind of thing that captains of industry or politicians thinking of tax revenues (i.e., all politicians) want us to reflect on and pay heed too! But, thrift is a virtue that is relevant also to non tartan-skirted folks."

— **Dr. Stanley Carlson-Theis,**
Senior Policy Director, Center for Public Justice

"For most of us, thrift is the necessary precondition to generosity. In this book, Dr. Malloch points out the public as well as private benefits of the twin virtues of thrift and generosity. Both societies and individuals yearn to influence history, and this engaging book illustrates the simple truth that we must be good stewards, not merely consumers, of the gifts entrusted to us if we hope to make a positive impact on those around us."

— **Colin A. Hanna,** Executive Director, Let Freedom Ring

"Wow…, has Ted Malloch packed a lot into this book on a much broader perspective than you could have ever guessed from its title.  It supports traditional thought while showing excellent research and examples. It proves the thesis that thrift results in many kinds of wealth.  I had to read and study it a second time to appreciate the depth of thinking here exhibited!"

— **Milt Kuyers,** CEO, Faustel, Inc.

"Dr. Theodore Malloch's book on thrift reminds us of the importance of this overlooked virtue by tracing its value, both historic and contemporary. Tracing its roots from the Scottish enlightenment to the no-waste credo of Sam Walton, Malloch shows how thrift advantages others rather than ourselves, a noble act that can make us happier. Equally important, thrift provides the resources to stimulate prosperity: without savings there is no investment. Indeed, Malloch argues persuasively that underdevelopment is a moral dilemma because corruption and ineptitude have crowded out thrift. This important book is lively, topical, and immediately useful."

—**Dr. Paul Zak,** Professor of Economics and Director, Center for Neuroeconomics Studies, Claremont Graduate University and Editor of *Moral Markets: The Critical Role of Values in the Economy*

"In an earlier era, America's Calvinist president, Calvin Coolidge, argued that industry, thrift, and self-control are not sought because they create wealth, but because they create character. Malloch's treatment of thrift needs to be read aloud in classrooms so that once again our people will find and build character."

— **Paul Corts,** President, CCCU

"*Thrift* takes on 'the crucial linkage between democracy, freedom and capital.' Ted Malloch asks the tough questions and goes deep to find the truths, which animate our lives. His thoughts and conclusions on 'spiritual capital' are especially persuasive."

— **Al Sikes,** Chairman, Trinity Forum

"As an Aberdonian, from the north of Scotland, I can certainly appreciate the virtue of thrift more than most. Thrift as well as other traditional Scottish virtues such as enterprise, hard work and innovation has helped the Scots build up many successful global businesses particularly in the financial arena. This book shows wonderfully how that was possible."

—**Bev Hendry,** President, Aberdeen Asset Management

*(Continued)*

"The word thrift seems decidedly unmodern, a fusty old term redolent of Victorian or even Puritan strictness, or perhaps hypocrisy. As this book shows, it is anything but: it is intimately tied to developments such as the economic rise of China and the other Asian tigers, and to many of the ills that plague modern America. Ted Malloch's marvelous book roots an understanding of thrift in philosophy, economics and theology and shows how this virtue is vital to the renewal of our lives and societies."

**—Dr. Paul Marshall,**
Senior Fellow, The Hudson Institute

"If America is to prevail in today's global economy, we will need to cultivate the virtues Ted Malloch describes in this brilliant and extremely readable book. It is wisdom on steroids."

**—Joseph Shattan,**
author of *Architects of Victory: Six Heroes of the Cold War*

"Whether a forgotten virtue or not, Malloch makes compelling argument that thrift is a virtue that is very much its own reward. And the reward is not only, or most importantly, in the form of material wealth. Thrift is part of a package of virtues, such as discipline, accountability and farsightedness, that are necessary to a satisfying and meaningful life, and in most cases sufficient as well."

**—Dwight Lee**,
Ramsay Professor of Economics and Private Enterprise,
Terry School of Business, University of Georgia

"Thrift is often negatively associated with miserliness. Rooted in the verb 'to thrive', however, it is actually about human flourishing. Thrifty people are future-minded, prepared to delay gratification in the hope of a better tomorrow. A wealth of new research affirms the importance of this characteristic for human happiness. Against a background of over consumption based on debt-based instant gratification, Ted Malloch's book provides a compelling case for the recovery of thrift as a practical virtue relevant to every social sphere. The author's vast experience of many of these areas ensures that this book is not only timely but firmly based in contemporary reality."

—**Dr. Peter S. Heslam,**
Director of Transforming Business,
University of Cambridge

# Thrift

## REBIRTH
## OF A FORGOTTEN VIRTUE

THEODORE ROOSEVELT MALLOCH

ENCOUNTER BOOKS  NEW YORK • LONDON

First American edition published in 2009 by Encounter Books,
an activity of Encounter for Culture and Education, Inc.,
a nonprofit, tax exempt corporation.
Encounter Books website address: www.encounterbooks.com

Manufactured in the United States and printed on
acid-free paper. The paper used in this publication meets
the minimum requirements of ANSI/NISO Z39.48– 1992
(R 1997) (Permanence of Paper).

FIRST AMERICAN EDITION

LIBRARY OF CONGRESS CATALOGING-IN-PUBLICATION DATA

Malloch, Theodore R.
Thrift : rebirth of a forgotten virtue / by Theodore Roosevelt Malloch.
p. cm.

Includes bibliographical references and index.
ISBN-13: 978-1-59403-260-8 (pbk. : alk. paper)
ISBN-10: 1-59403-260-2 (pbk. : alk. paper)
1. Thriftiness.
2. Finance, Personal. I. Title.

HG179.M35 2009

332.024—dc22

2009018979

*For Scotland,*
*the Scots,*
*those in the Scottish diaspora,*
*and all who share the ideals of the Scottish Enlightenment*

# CONTENTS

# FOREWORD

In my lifetime, stretching back nearly a century now, we have witnessed a thousandfold increase in scientific knowledge and material and technological advances few thought possible. In the realm of spiritual information and of deep wisdom, we have not yet made comparable advances. This is likely to be a central challenge for extending progress in this new century.

Thrift is a timeless quality with spiritual implications. It is imperative that all societies learn to save, *not* just spend. I started out poor, but through the principles of thrift and hard work, I was able to get ahead. When I married, my wife and I set a goal of saving 50 percent of our income. We avoided consumer debt—in fact, we bought our first home with cash. We carried this "thrifty" approach into later life. Once I even bought a Rolls Royce, but I bought it used!

I believe in working hard and often put in almost 60 hours a week. I tend to agree with J. Paul Getty, whose motto was *"Make your money first...then think about spending it."* In my career as an investor, I have always thought it is also wise to shop for what I called Value Investments. I always followed the fundamental "bargain-hunting" approach to investing. This long-range view requires patience. My Templeton Growth Fund, which I ran for 50 years, held stocks for an average six to seven years. I always searched for companies around the world that offered both low prices and an excellent long-term outlook. It's not easy, but if you're going to buy the best bargains, you need to look in more than one industry, and look in more than one nation.

After many years of observation, I feel it curious that thrift has become a more and more neglected value in our society; we seem to be practicing it less and less and thinking about it even less. What does this mean for the future of our society? Take the influential generation known as the Baby Boomers. Their public image is one of affluence and upward mobility, but *U.S. News & World Report* says that a quarter of all professional and managerial Boomers have a negative net worth and are teetering on the edge of personal bankruptcy. Despite their emphasis on family values, political correctness, and even traditional virtues, most Baby Boomers are not very thrifty. In fact, thrift has become America's "lost or forgotten virtue," rarely mentioned and never celebrated, despite its true historical significance. But it is an important American core value, one that has shaped and in some ways continues to shape our national character. To some, thrift may seem like an occasional means-imposed necessity rather than a route to joy. But if we took the time to learn about the virtue of thrift, to study its ways in combination with gratitude and generosity, it could lead to deep, lasting contentment, and many people would be better off, spiritually and financially.

The qualities that distinguish thriftiness from mere cheapness are noteworthy. Thrift is part of wisdom. Thrift and gratitude, thrift and ethical standards, and thrift and hard work all go hand in hand. The Bible, literature, poetry, and philosophy, as well as examples from daily life and most faith traditions, demonstrate that thrift is more than just understanding the bottom line. Indeed, thrift is part of a religious and cultural understanding of how we use our time, our talents, and our resources. As inherently virtuous as thrifty living is, its capacity for leading to deep joy is severely limited if its goals are merely self-serving. On the other hand, when thrift is combined with the virtue of generosity, when empathy opens the doors for channeling the thriftiness to generosity, the potential for good is greatly magnified.

One of my friends suggests that "the safest way to double your money is to fold it over once and put it in your pocket." Plus thrift and generosity do go together. There is a wonderful law of nature that the three things we crave the most in life—happiness, freedom, and peace of mind—are always obtained by giving them to someone else.

I remain the eternal optimist: Although once I may have been a Wall Street titan, I now devote my life, enthusiasm, and fortune to enriching people's lives by investing in the greatest treasure—spiritual wealth.

**Sir John M. Templeton**
Lyford Cay, the Bahamas 2007

*"Thrift is essential to well-ordered living."*
—John D. Rockefeller

In the center of Rockefeller Center in New York City is a polished block of marble inscribed with a single word. The stone is the keystone of the complex, but it is little noticed, and no wonder, because this keystone is dwarfed by everything around it. Built during the Great Depression, Rockefeller Center is itself a monument to the wealth and power of John D. Rockefeller, whose private fortune, adjusted for inflation, remains the single largest ever amassed in American history. At his fortune's peak, Rockefeller personally controlled nearly 2 percent of the American economy. The office towers soar above the towers of St. Patrick's Cathedral across the street, and the courtyard at their base is a lavish display of fountains, gardens, fine shops, and, of course, the famous skating rink, behind which the great Christmas tree is placed each year. Nearby, the studios of NBC add a final polish of celebrity and glamour.

Nearly lost in the opulence is the keystone engraved with the single word

# THRIFT

What, a visitor today may wonder, does "thrift" have to do with this grand setting? For thrift is a forgotten virtue, much as the keystone motto of Rockefeller Center is the forgotten center of the complex.

Thanks to globalization, new technologies, and deregulation, among other forces, we live in a new era of affluence. Like the keystone, the virtue of thrift is almost totally obscured by the wealth and prosperity of our era, and the ensuing sense of entitlement. These days no one wants to be considered a *cheapskate*. Frugality is about as popular as chastity. But it wasn't always so. A recent, and telltale, Yahoo word search on *thrift* produced few results: a newsletter on "simple living," an offensive guide called *Cheap Stingy Bastard*, on so-called good deals, *The Complete Tightwad Gazette*, the somewhat satirical *Cheapskate Monthly*, numerous addresses for actual thrift shops, and the frugal *tip* of the week—things like saving aluminum cans. This is not the virtuous thrift of an earlier and more respectful era.

I have conducted a very *un*scientific and admittedly utterly biased sample (just like most sociological surveys) over the past year or so of the people I know and have met around the country. Some I know well, many are simply acquaintances, but most are new folks I don't know at all. I ask them what they think of thrift. I don't tell them I am writing about it or studying it. I just want to gauge their reaction and response. Half of this modest sample gives me a confused look meaning: Are you crazy? What the hell is thrift? They have no conception of the word, its history or lineage. Frankly, they could care less. About 30 percent of the people say, Oh yeah, thrifty, that's cheap, right? Well,

I am not cheap. They have a pejorative or quite negative response to the term. They are running away from thrift. About 15 percent of people admit that they know what thrift is, although they still associate it with cheapness, and while they wouldn't want to publicize it or broadcast it to everyone, they are, well, cheap on occasion. This dirty little secret is something they want kept secret, but they are rather proud of it. This leaves about 5 percent of people, mostly highly educated and having above-average wealth, some even learned with multiple degrees or regular worshippers in whatever church or synagogue, who admit to knowing what thrift is, appreciating it, practicing it, and in some cases even naming it as a good thing or a virtue. Only 5 percent of people (in this biased survey, apologies to my friend George Gallup) have not forgotten the virtue of thrift.

What have the others forgotten? Modern definitions of thrift are not nearly as good as the 1828 one provided by Noah Webster himself:

> Economical in the use or appropriation of money, goods or provisions of any kind; saving unnecessary expense, either of money or any thing else which is to be used or consumed; sparing; not profuse, prodigal or lavish. We ought to be frugal not only in the expenditure of money and of goods, but in the employment of time. Prudent economy; good husbandry or housewifery; a sparing use or appropriation of money or commodities; a judicious use of any thing to be expended or employed; that careful management

which expends nothing unnecessarily, and applies what is used to a profitable purpose; nothing is wasted. It is not equivalent to parsimony,
the latter being an excess to a fault. Thrift is always a virtue.[1]

While the social historian Gertrude Himmelfarb was
certainly correct in describing the transmutation of virtues to values[2] as part of the general de-moralization of
society, she was less complete about the religious origin
of some of the key Victorian virtues, such as thrift. The
Victorian contributions and moral framework, in both
Britain and in America, were, as she noted, essential, not
only for the good life of individuals but also for the well-
being of society. But where did this seemingly foreign,
now distant notion of thrift originate? And how is it related to the American preference for what has come to be
curiously known as fiscal conservatism? We need make
mention at the outset that there is a connection between
thrift and thriving. This is an important key to the theme
of this book.  That thrift helps us thrive is again a vitally
useful point to make in offsetting the gravitational pull of
so many of its pejorative connotations.

Fiscal conservatism—the public face of thrift—is a
term used today to refer to an economic and political policy that advocates restraint of government taxation, government expenditures and deficits, and government debt.
In an earlier era this tendency was known as public thrift,
because thrift was said to have *both* a public and a private

side. A major cause of the American Revolution  was "No Taxation without Representation." Americans insisted that their historic rights as Britons entitled them to a voice in setting tax policies, which the government in Britain denied. The issue was not the tax itself or its size, but the fact that it was imposed without the consent of those it affected.

The Democratic-Republican Party of Thomas Jefferson supported a weak central government and a more *laissez-faire* approach than that of Alexander Hamilton's rival party, the Federalists. They opposed Hamilton's plan for the federal government to pay off the debts owed by the states for the expense of the American Revolution, because some of the debt was held by financiers and speculators (who did not deserve payment) rather than the original holders. Hamilton got his legislation passed and set taxes to pay the debts. Jefferson strongly opposed having any national debt, although he relented when the opportunity came in 1803 to purchase the territory of Louisiana.

James Madison, James Monroe, and John Quincy Adams were elected by the Democratic-Republican Party, but after the fiscal disasters of the War of 1812, they came to support most of the Federalist position, realizing that the nation needed a central bank and a steady income flow from tariffs. In the mid-1800s, a new fiscal conservative political party emerged, the Republican Party. Unlike the modern fiscal conservatives, these fiscal conservatives were supporters of protectionism and tariffs. In the early 1900s, fiscal conservatives were often at odds with progressive President Theodore Roosevelt, particularly for his support of antitrust laws.

During the 1920s, President Calvin Coolidge's pro-business economic policies were credited for the successful period of economic growth known as the "Roaring Twenties." After the great crash of 1929, however, Coolidge's policies, and then Hoover's, took the blame. Coolidge not only lowered taxes but also reduced the national debt from World War I. His actions, however, may have been due more to a sense of federalism than fiscal conservatism: Many noted that, as governor of Massachusetts, Coolidge supported wages and hours legislation, opposed child labor, imposed economic controls during World War I, favored safety measures in factories and even worker representation on corporate boards. If he did not support these measures while president, it was because in the 1920s such matters were considered the responsibilities of state and local governments.

During the 1930s Franklin Roosevelt's New Deal was opposed by many conservatives because it expanded the scope of the federal government and regulated the economy. In general, Roosevelt did not raise taxes above the high levels Hoover had set. But he spent liberally to move the country out of its deep economic travail. Roosevelt's Treasury secretary, Henry Morgenthau, believed in balanced budgets, stable currency, reduction of the national debt, and the need for more private investment. He accepted Roosevelt's double budget as legitimate—that is, a balanced regular budget and an "emergency" budget for agencies such as the WPA (Works Projects Administration), the PWA (Public Works Administration), and the CCC (Civilian

Conservative Corps) that would be temporary until full recovery was at hand. He fought against the veterans' bonus until Congress finally overrode Roosevelt's veto and gave out two billion dollars in 1936. Morgenthau's most notable but also controversial achievement was the new Social Security program: he managed to reverse the proposals to fund it from general revenue and insisted it be funded by new taxes on employees.

In World War II there was broad agreement in favor of heavy taxes, with conservatives insisting that the income tax base be broadened to include the great majority, rather than the 10 percent who before 1942 paid all income taxes. America was at war, and we had to foot the bill.

Fiscal conservatism was most loudly and rhetorically promoted during the presidency of Ronald Reagan from 1981 to 1989. During his tenure, Reagan touted economic policies that became known as Reaganomics. Based on supply-side economics, Reagan's policies cut income taxes, raised Social Security taxes, deregulated the economy, and instituted a tight monetary policy to stop inflation. Reagan favored reducing the size and scope of government, sought a limited government, and proposed a balanced federal budget.

Conservatism of the fiscal sort has had its supporters and detractors throughout just about all of American history. Unfortunately, some of the Republicans who ran on its premises when in office did more to grow the bureaucracy and big government than even their opponents. Except for Margaret Thatcher's Britain, few countries have had an ongoing public debate in political circles about public thrift, the size and cost of government or balanced budgets, let alone the rivalry between the individual and the all-powerful State.

On a communal and personal level Americans seem predisposed to policies of thrift in their personal as well as their civic lives. Behaviorally, however, they often act, spend, and vote quite differently. And when things are going gangbusters, all focus is on spending and consumerism, not thrift. But when recession strikes, out from under the floor resurfaces that odd virtue, thrift, as in: I should have saved more and consumed less. Why is my credit card so problematic to pay down? Was I forced to charge yet more "stuff"? What is it about thrift, public or private, that makes it so hard to achieve? Does it necessarily contradict or oppose economic growth? Where did it originate, anyway? Is it really a lost and forgotten virtue? Is that necessarily a bad thing?

## CHAPTER ONE

# The Origins of Thrift

*"Thrift comes too late when you find it*
*at the bottom of your purse."*
—Seneca

Thrift is associated not only with the Scottish people but also, more specifically, with the Calvinist religion, which has, over the centuries, exerted a powerful influence on their Gaelic culture and customs. It was Max Weber, the father of German sociology, who first saw the importance of Calvinism in the rise of the modern capitalist economy. And it is by returning to the Calvinist tradition that we will discover the element that Weber missed—the nature of thrift as a virtue.

Calvinism was a religious response to the needs and concerns of a newly rising sixteenth-century middle class. The foresighted use of funds had become necessary in a society that had risen above bare subsistence and in which people were engaged extensively in the practice of trade and manufacturing. The theological position, where worth is determined less by the amount one spends than by the wisdom with which one discharges responsibilities as a steward of God's creation, is ingrained in the Reformation. But the position is far older, and can be traced back to the saga of the patriarch Abraham, where in Isaiah 51:2 it is recorded, *"Look to Abraham your father, and to Sarah who bore you; for I called him alone, and blessed him, and increased him."* Thrift is one of the lessons taught in the great story of Joseph in the Old Testament, which concerns husbandry in all its forms. And much of the power of Reformation thinking lay in its ability to revive the story of Israel and apply it directly to the sentiments of the new middle class.

Calvin's *Institutes of the Christian Religion*[1] and his many *Commentaries*[2] are replete with interpretation of scripture about nearly every doctrine. The virtue of thrift plays prominently throughout the entire corpus of his work. His reading of Matthew 6 is particularly noteworthy in this regard. Believers ought to rely on God's Fatherly care, to expect that He will bestow upon them whatever they feel necessary, and not to torment themselves by unnecessary anxiety. Calvin forbids believers to be anxious or to seek in a manner that looks around and about them, without looking at God, on whom *alone* their eyes ought to be fixed. Calvin says, "Beware those who are never at ease, but when they have before their eyes an abundance of provisions; and who, not admitting that the protection of the world belongs to God, fret and tease themselves with perpetual uneasiness."[3]

By seeking *first* the Kingdom of God, Calvin argues for another restraint on excessive anxiety. He states, "It is a gross and indolent neglect of the soul, and of the heavenly life"[4] that leads men to fail and moderate their cares and desires. In a renowned passage, Calvin extols the "lay

not up" treasures on earth phraseology with a fiery warning. "This deadly plague regains everywhere throughout the
world. Men are grown mad with an insatiable desire of gain.
Christ charges them with folly, in collecting wealth with
great care, and then giving up their happiness to moths and
to rust, or exposing it as a prey to thieves…They are blind
and destitute of sound judgment, who give themselves so
much toil and uneasiness in amassing wealth, which is li-
able to putrefaction, or robbery, or a thousand other acci-
dents: particularly when God allows us a place in heaven for
laying up a treasure, and kindly invites us to enjoy riches
which never perish."[5]

The notion of *daily bread* that sustains us and the labor
involved in providing such sustenance, built into the very
structure of creation, is highlighted continually by Calvin.
"Yet our Lord commenced with bread and the supports of
an earthly life, that from such a beginning he might carry us
higher."[6] Calvin is teaching his followers to endure patiently,
to accept humility and not to be "intoxicated by a false confidence in earthly abundance."[7] This understanding of thrift is
radically different from Dickensian caricatures like Ebenezer
Scrooge. For Calvin, "our bread" is a metaphor for *all* goods
and belongings. But these are not literally *our* bread. Calvin
states, "It is so called, not because it belongs to us by right,
but because the fatherly kindness of God has set it apart for
our use. It becomes ours, because our heavenly Father freely
bestows it on us for the supplies of our necessities. The fields
must no doubt be cultivated, labor must be bestowed on
gathering the fruits of the earth, and every man must submit
to the toil of his calling, in order to procure food. But all this

does not hinder us from being fed by the undeserved kindness of God, without which men might waste their strength
to no purpose. We are thus taught, that what we seem to
have acquired by our own industry is His *gift*."[8]

Caring for God's endowment in a respectful and thrifty
fashion is here a form of biblical obedience. Some would
contrast this with Francis Bacon's notion that the world is
ours to exploit. Calvin actually taught that the command-
ment in the first chapters of Genesis would instruct us to
"build and to keep," which suggests a proper balance, not a
mandate to pillage. And this brings me to the crucial point:
Thrift is not merely a matter of accumulating wisely; it is
also a matter of spending wisely. And the underlying motive
is not greed but *gratitude:* gratitude to God for the gifts he
has bestowed, which leads us to give of them in turn. And
this gratitude to God is something that we spread through
society through our prudent stewardship. Thrift is not only
an individual virtue. It also gives rise to a social condition
in which the love of neighbor informs each person's use of
his possessions.

The Reformers understood the sin of greed to be a sin
directly against one's neighbor. Their understanding presumed the sin of greed to be in the category of those sins
that cause a break in the relation between neighbor and self.
The theory of economic scarcity rather than abundance,
upon which these theological claims rest, may indeed be
very outdated. But for the Reformers, the sin in question
was a transgression of the limit set for us in the world by
God as creator, the consequence of which is a struggle of

sovereignty over *who* is really in control of our lives and our future. Hence the sin of greed is really the sin of "desiring a life subject to human control over a life of vulnerable trust"[9] in God. The Puritan divine Richard Baxter puts it: "Frugality or sparing is an act of fidelity, obedience, and gratitude, by which we use all our estates so faithfully for the chief Owner, so obediently to our chief Ruler, and so gratefully to our chief Benefactor, as that we waste it not any other way."

It is significant that the Calvinist worldview, and its particular notion of thrift, found hospitable acceptance in only a few European countries where the Reformation firmly took hold—in Scotland, the Netherlands, and Switzerland, and of course later in the Bay colony of Massachusetts and eventually as part of the American experience. Protestantism began in 1517 with a "protest," hence the name, when Martin Luther, a German Augustinian monk, nailed *95 Theses* to a church door in Wittenberg. What started as the spiritual doubts of one monk spiraled into a religious movement. Luther, a gifted scholar, returned to the text of the Bible and rejected the Church's practices that were not written therein. He interpreted the Bible as the literal word of God and rejected the authority of the Pope, an action that had previously led to a charge of heresy followed by burning at the stake. However, Luther was given time to reconsider his so-called heretical views, which he did, before deciding that he had to stay faithful to his conscience. In his own words, "Here I stand." Fortunately for Luther, various German princes ensured his survival and funded the propagation of his theories and doctrines through the new printing press. Soon Lutheran texts were spread across Europe, fanning the flames of religious conflict and inciting rebellion throughout Christendom.

Scotland took the Reformed path and sided with the protesters. It became the seat and symbol of thrift, and the image sticks, so that today the cheapest rental car company is named Thrifty and uses a Scotsman wearing a kilt as its logo. There are Scottish (discount) Inns and a dozen other instances exploiting the reputation of this flinty but commercially minded people. Religion was very important to Scots in the sixteenth century, and the Church was crucial to all aspects of everyday life. It was responsible for education, health, welfare, and discipline. It was also very important on an individual level. The Church was the vehicle for expressing inner spirituality, and changes to its forms of worship could endanger one's chances of salvation.

The Reformation split the Church into Catholic and Protestant factions, creating two roads to salvation, both of which claimed to be the sole way of reaching it. So it was very important to people that the Scottish state choose to travel down the right road. When Lutheran books in *Latin* started to appear in Scotland, the radical message, which they carried quickly, made a strong impression on many Scots, and, although King James V tried to ban their distribution, print always had the knack of avoiding the censor.

In the early sixteenth century, Scotland was a piously Catholic nation. But its very devoutness meant that an increasingly educated populace sought more personal forms of spiritual experience. Rome and its doctrines, it seemed, were not always congenial to a nation heading at high speed for the modern world. Reform was in the air, but only a tiny minority at this stage favored Protestantism and a complete break with Rome.

After Henry VIII converted to Protestantism, taking most of the English nation with him, James V, in need of money to support his royal court's extravagant lifestyle, cunningly flirted with Protestant ideas in order to scare the Pope into granting him tax concessions. However, in 1542 James V died; his only heir was the infant Mary, Queen of Scots. Scotland was plunged into a crisis the likes of which hadn't been seen before.

Both France and England pursued the opportunity to commandeer the Scottish throne by tying the young queen to them through marriage. England was Protestant, France was Catholic. In their bitter power struggle over Scotland the issue of Scotland's faith became not merely a question of religious denomination but one of international power politics. The "Rough Wooing,," as it came to be called, saw England attempt to force Mary's hand through repeated invasions and the defeat of the Scottish army at the Battle of Pinkie. In return, the French supplied the Scots with troops and the firepower to resist Henry's advances. Both sides spent a fortune on this wooing of the Scots. It is thought that Henry VIII perhaps spent all that he had gained from the dissolution of England's monasteries on the campaigns, though to no avail. In the end the French triumphed, though briefly, as it turned out.

While the Church of Scotland traces its roots back to the earliest Christians in Scotland, who came to the

Isle of Iona on the western shore, its identity was principally shaped by the Scottish Reformation of 1560. At that
point, the Church in Scotland finally broke with Rome, in
a process of Protestant reform led, among others, by the fiery John Knox. It reformed its doctrines and government,
drawing on the principles of John Calvin, which Knox
had been exposed to while living in Switzerland. In 1560,
the Scottish Parliament abolished papal jurisdiction and
approved Calvin's Confession of Faith, but it did not accept many of the principles laid out in Knox's *First Book of
Discipline*, which argued, among other things, that all of the
assets of the old Church should pass to the new. The 1560
Reformation Settlement was not ratified by the crown for
some years, and the question of church government also
remained unresolved. By 1572 the Acts of 1560 were finally approved by the young James VI, but the Concordat of
Leith also allowed the crown to appoint bishops with the
church's approval. John Knox himself had no clear views on
the office of bishop, preferring to see bishops renamed as
"superintendents," but in response to the new Concordat
a Presbyterian party emerged headed by Andrew Melville,
author of the *Second Book of Discipline*.

Melville and his supporters enjoyed some temporary successes, most notably in the Golden Act of 1592,
which gave parliamentary approval to Presbyterian courts.
However, King James, by skillful manipulation of both
church and state, steadily reintroduced parliamentary and
then diocesan Episcopacy. By the time he died in 1625, the
Church of Scotland had a full panel of bishops and archbish-
ops. General Assemblies, moreover, met only at times and

places approved by the crown. The Scottish Reformation transformed Scotland, modernizing its ways and opening its economy. But its single largest contribution was in the realm of freedom—from Rome and Church edict.

It was precisely in the context of this new free economy that the Calvinist virtues flourished, for they were exactly what the Scots needed in order to take advantage of their new situation and spread their prosperity. Thrift, as understood by the Calvinist tradition, was on a par with the two cardinal virtues of prudence and temperance. It is worth making even more of the connection between thrift and prudence than most have made of it. Temperance is more obvious. Prudence arrived on the scene with trumpets as the Siamese twin of thrift, or perhaps even as the mother of thrift. I would not call it a tame lion; it is better called a well-trained horse. By linking thrift with prudence, the reader will later see how this connection reinforces the argument of later chapters in this book.

Thrift was not seen as a matter of stinginess or hoarding, both of which exhibit the perversion of property and the failure to put it to a creative use. Nor did it demand a retreat from risk or an avoidance of magnanimous gestures. Thrift was seen as a matter of the wise use of assets— accumulating where this was possible, investing where this promised a return, and avoiding waste. Thrift was nothing more or less than wise stewardship, conducted under the eyes of God. And it was exactly what the capitalist economy required: Scotland in the seventeenth century did not merely join the modern world; it played its own special part in creating it.

Scottish migration to America began just after the outset of the Reformation, and as a result Calvinism was transported to fertile soil. The *Mayflower Compact* shows the Puritans at their best, making a (Calvinistic) covenant with God in the New Land. At the beginning of the twentieth century in America there was something of a revival, likely originating in one of our many evangelical Great Awakenings and certainly influenced by the earlier Calvinism of Jonathan Edwards, Cotton Mather, and other preachers in New England. It too fused religious feeling with thrift. The poet Charles Fillmore penned a famous poem in 1915 that summed up this train of thought. It is still remembered for its first line, which manages to weave financial and spiritual images so perfectly as to present saving and salvation as a single idea:

> *The Lord is my banker; my credit is good.*
>
> *He maketh me to lie down in the consciousness of omnipresent abundance;*
>
> *He giveth me the key to His strongbox.*
>
> *He restoreth my faith in His riches;*
>
> *He guideth me in the paths of prosperity for His Name's sake.*
>
> *Yea, though I walk in the very shadow of debt, I shall fear no evil, for Thou art with me;*
>
> *Thy silver and Thy gold, they secure me.*
>
> *Thou preparest a way for me in the presence of the collector;*

*Thou fillest my wallet with plenty; my measure
runneth over.*

*Surely goodness and plenty will follow me all the
days of my life,*

*And I shall do business in the name of the Lord forever.*

Capitalism is a game, all right. Dierdre McCloskey's book
*Bourgeois Virtues* claims that it is in fact what she calls a
Good Person's Game.[10] But the book also claims that playing such a game can make you good. She takes the next step
of apologizing for capitalism and the bourgeois life. Her
argument sees the game as essentially a cooperative game,
largely a conversation, which to fulfill its purpose requires
all the seven virtues—the four cardinal virtues recognized
since ancient times (courage, prudence temperance, and
justice), and the three theological virtues (faith, hope, and
charity), added by St Paul.

In Chapter 3 I will explore the theory of virtue in more
depth. But this preliminary discussion enables us to say exactly why thrift, as the Calvinist tradition understood it, is
a virtue on a par with the seven generally recognized. Thrift
is opposed to two prevalent human vices—profligacy and
meanness. The first wastes resources, the second fails to use
them. Thrift is a habit of wise stewardship, which preserves
resources while also putting them to use. It is a vital instrument of economic well-being and a source of human happiness. Without thrift there is no provision for the future,
and property becomes precarious, arbitrary, and vulnerable
to predation and waste. Thrift therefore makes possible
both long-term economic planning and the building of

families and charitable institutions. It underlies every form of public spirit, plus the habit of giving to strangers, which is one of the supreme achievements of the Protestant tradition—still to be witnessed here in America but vanishing, under the impact of socialism and the welfare state, from Scotland today.

Before moving on, however, it is worth paying a tribute to Max Weber, whose connection of the spirit of capitalism with the Protestant ethic first opened the discussion on which I have been building my argument. And the best tribute to pay to this great sociologist is to suggest why he was wrong. Weber's treatment of the Protestant Reformation[11] is actually based on confusing the sin of greed with the virtue of thrift. Weber looked at the coincidence of wealth in the Reformed countries and concluded that a certain kind of theology seemed to breed persons who did not desire enjoyment but instead preferred gain. While it is true that Northern Europeans and their emigrants to North America worked to meet basic needs and in the course of this accumulated savings, the reason for this has less to do with greed than with work. In Calvinism, for the first time, work was given a religious character and became an ethical demand. A person worked not to live, but because God commanded it.

The *calling* and *vocation* of a person was, in the Calvinist view of things, a mark of that person's election or non-election by God. Work showed evidence of productivity, as demonstrated in the parable of the talents, rather than an appetite for pleasure. Weber concluded that the result of all this working hard and spending little was saving, and that saving was always in search of new and appreciating investments. But unlike the Calvin Weber described, the other parts of Calvin espoused a different relationship between human beings and the things they possessed, a kind of communitarian understanding of what they had and held. Geneva was actually flooded by poor refugees for this generous reason. Calvin believed that as the rich had a responsibility to the poor, so too did the poor have a mission to the rich. The poor were the receivers of God, the vicars of Christ, the solicitors of God who offered the rich an opportunity to rid themselves from monetary slavery, an opportunity to be saved from greed.

Weber was thus only half right in connecting Calvin's thought to the accumulation of riches and the later evolution of capitalism. For what Calvin advocated in his day was not that men should be rich in goods and so greedy, but that they should be rich toward God and so generous. He did not legislate generosity in a strict calculation or a defined sum but rather called followers to take the *rule of love* as their guide. This was no form of asceticism but rather a life of thrift as a lived virtue. It was also a life of gratitude, for all that men had been given was not theirs merely to have or keep but to hold and employ as stewards until, in Calvin's words, "such time as they came to behold the face of Him whose love had never let them go."[12] The meaning invested in the idea of religious calling, first by Luther in a simplified form, and then in a systematic form by Calvin, should therefore be understood in terms of gratitude.

The Scots often looked to their French counterparts for answers to philosophical queries. France was enjoying its Age of Enlightenment, and quickly the intellectual fire spread to Scotland. Although sharing the French speculative-rationalist spirit, the work of the considerable band of Scottish philosophers was tempered with doses of skepticism and a more pronounced form of utilitarianism, or what has come to be known as Scottish Realism. Unlike the French, the Scottish thinkers were particularly concerned with economic growth and development, the consequences of international trade and the mechanics of an emerging urban, commercial, property-owning society—concerns reflecting the reality of post-1707 after the unification of Scotland and England.

The Scottish Enlightenment stretched from about 1740 to 1790, for fifty years. Unlike the Enlightenment in France, many if not most of its protagonists were academics. Francis Hutcheson, Adam Smith, Thomas Reid, and John Millar were professors at the University of Glasgow. Adam Ferguson, Dugald Stewart, and William Robertson were at the University of Edinburgh. The universities of Aberdeen and St. Andrews were dominated by their students and followers. But there were also some important figures outside the academy who influenced the course of the dialogue, including Lord Kames, Sir James Steuart, the medical doctor James Anderson, and, above everyone else, the towering figure of David Hume.

Hume's view of ethics as part of the metabolism of self-preservation was turned upside down by Francis Hutcheson, who argued that virtue yields pleasure because it conforms to our natural and innate moral sense, while vice yields pain because it is unnatural. As a result, Hutcheson came up with the more utilitarian ethical precepts that the height of virtue was achieving the greatest good for the greatest number. Adam Smith, his student, attempted to reconcile the Hume and Hutcheson positions using the artifice of what he called "natural sympathy" and the "impartial spectator." He also spoke powerfully to the rising commercial and trade questions that Scotland was witnessing in reaction to mercantilism, the argument that international trade is unchangeable.

The Scots came up with meta-sociological accounts of the natural progress of civilization. This natural history approach was initiated by David Hume. A kind of conjectural history suggested that there were distinct stages in economic history. Adam Ferguson, John Millar, and Adam Smith were the leading proponents of this line of thinking. Smith envisaged history as progressing through four economic stages, each attended by political and social structures: a hunting and gathering stage, a pastoral and nomadic stage, an agricultural and feudalist stage, and the final commerce and manufacturing stage, which Scotland was entering. Like Ferguson, Smith placed division of labor and the expansion of commerce as the fundamental drivers of history. So important were these efforts of the Scottish Enlightenment School that Voltaire himself noted that "we look to Scotland for all our ideas of civilization."

Adam Smith, the Glasgow professor of moral philosophy and the father of economics, is still venerated for his 1776 tome, *The Wealth of Nations*. The *invisible hand* so regularly appearing in Smithian doctrine is in fact none other than the Providence of (Calvin's) God. Smith, make no mistake, was fully a child of the Scottish Enlightenment and reacted to the literalism and stringency of dour Scottish Calvinism. But he was born into its culture and surrounded by its legacy. What is less well known at this juncture is the tie between his emerging theory and empirical findings concerning capitalistic economies and his earlier moral thinking.

In 1759, 17 years before the publication of *The Wealth of Nations,* Smith had published a classic moral treatise called *The Theory of Moral Sentiments.* Very much a product of the Scottish Enlightenment, this book articulated a set of coherent thoughts that tied the head to the heart and laid the framework that undergirds all his economics. For Smith, economics and ethics cannot and should not be decoupled. The economy depends on trust, and that trust is both embedded in the virtues of the individual and contracted in the rule of law in any given (commercial) society.

Broadly speaking, Smith followed the views of his mentor, Francis Hutcheson, who divided moral philosophy into four parts: Ethics and Virtue, Private rights and Natural liberty, Familial rights (called Oeconomicks), and State and Individual rights (called Politicks). More specifically, Smith divided moral systems into categories of the nature of morality, which included Propriety, Prudence, and Benevolence, and categories of the motive of morality, which included Self-love, Reason, and Sentiment. Smith embarks on a concluding, climactic Section III, "Of Self-Command," which was, for him, the master virtue. "The man who acts according to the rules of perfect prudence, of strict justice, and of proper benevolence may be said to be perfectly virtuous." Here is Smith's wise statement from that original treatment summing up his theory:

> Wise and judicious conduct, when directed to greater and nobler purposes than the care of the health, the fortune, the rank and reputation of the individual, is frequently and very properly called prudence. We talk of the prudence of the great general, of the great statesman, of the great legislator. Prudence is, in all these cases, combined with many greater and more splendid virtues, with valor, with extensive and strong benevolence, with a sacred regard to the rules of justice, and all these supported by a proper degree of self-command. This superior prudence, when carried to the highest degree of perfection, necessarily supposes the art, the talent, and the habit or disposition of acting with the most perfect propriety in every possible circumstance and situation. It necessarily supposes the utmost perfection of the entire intellectual and of all the moral virtues. It is the best head joined to the best heart. It is the most perfect wisdom combined with the most perfect virtue.

Contrast Smith with what *The Economist* recently said about economics: "If you want to avoid an argument over religion at your next dinner party, you might suppose it safe to invite an economist, sociologist, or two. They of all people could be expected to stick to Mammon." Well, maybe not. That proverbial *next* dinner party has shifted, and today we find new controversy surrounding the influence of religious belief and observance on economic growth, nation-building, and social progress. Far from dying or withering, as the positivists sought, religion today is an ever-present and growing force in the world. Secularization theories so popular in academe throughout the 1960s and 70s have come to look farcical.

Much of this new stirring revolves around a set of thoughts coming under the rubric *spiritual capital*. This still emerging concept builds on the recent research into social capital, which has shown that spirituality is a major factor in the formation of social networks, as well as an impetus for economic and social progress. There is growing recognition in the social sciences and, I should add, some policy circles as well that religion is not epiphenomenal. Neither is it fading away from public significance around the world. Indeed, it is a critical factor in understanding every facet of life, from the radius of trust to behavioral norms—all of which have vast economic, political, and social consequences.

Scholars such as Gary Becker and Robert Fogel, both Nobel Laureates in economics, have used the term "spiritual capital" to refer to that aspect of capital linked to religion and/or spirituality. The Harvard political scientist Robert Putnam's influential work on social capital found that religion is by far the largest generator of social capital, contributing more than half of all social capital. Its benefits to society are legion and stored for generations upon generations.

This is not the first time economists have held forth on this subject or considered the crossroads of economics and religion. It is exactly a century since Max Weber argued that northern Europe and America were made rich by the Protestant ethic. More recently Niall Ferguson, a British historian, has argued that the present economic stagnation in Germany and elsewhere in Europe owes much to the decline of religious belief and church attendance during the past four decades. Is the Protestant work ethic really dead? Does a latent cultural effect continue, and are thrift and related virtues central to the unfolding of that story?

In this book I will look at the effects of spiritual and religious practices, beliefs, networks, and institutions on individuals, communities, and societies, which have a thrift component. These are the guiding questions that will inform my discussion:

- To what extent should religion be considered in nation-building? In economic development? In the recovery of virtues such as thrift?

- Can one measure the state of national spirituality and make comparisons over time and across countries? How do such spiritual indices reflect the linkage between faith and action and between thrift and generosity?

- How do society, public policy, and the mediating structures (those entities between individual and the state) actively generate more spiritual capital? And how do they engender a renewal of virtues, including thrift?

And finally,

> • How are economic growth and social prog-
> ress linked to spiritual capital? Is saving—a
> key component in thrift—lost forever? If not,
> how can we make saving and conservation
> a part of sustainability, so as to end the con-
> sumption ethic?

The rules of engagement are: Each chapter will serve as
a catalyst for your thinking. After each chapter, take a
break and ponder the ramifications; engage with others in
a dialogue followed by questions and further comments
around the table, as equals. Read what other pundits are
saying and compare it with the news and opinion journals
you read. Look at the writings of leaders from think tanks,
academe, the media, and policy-making organizations.
Journalists are beginning to cover these topics and opine
on them, and websites are increasingly dedicated to them.
*Let the party begin!*

CHAPTER TWO

# Consumerism and Development

> *" By sowing frugality we reap liberty,*
> *a golden harvest. "*
>
> —Agesilaus II, King of Sparta

For the religious or spiritually inclined, insatiable desire is, as it was for Calvin and the Reformers, a source of unhappiness and even spiritual instability. Modern-day consumerists, however, have too often turned thrift on its head and made desire a source of liberation, where having more is the very definition of having arrived. Materialism unbridled has become synonymous with the "good life." The historian Christopher Lasch, in *The True and Only Heaven* (a phrase from Nathaniel Hawthorne), shows how capitalist moralists from the eighteenth century forward have made insatiable desire less and less of a vice and more and more of a virtue.[1] In one view, it is what drives the engine of economic growth and expansion. In consumer societies, virtues like thrift and self-denial are perceived as vices because they lead to economic stagnation. Thrifty people are called miserly and shriveled and unable to enjoy the fruits and pleasures of this life. True, thrift in itself does not produce wealth; but its opposite—profligacy—destroys wealth. The term "spendthrift," no longer in use, suggests a wasteful polar opposite to thrift. However, notions of restraint are no longer part of modern culture, nor is it now seen as shameful to enter into too much debt. One could even ask in our world of abundance if thrift has outlived its usefulness. The materialist who lives to consume would likely have to answer in the affirmative.

An expanding economy, it is said, is impeded by virtues such as thrift but thrives precisely on avid consumers who know *no* limits to their desire. In such a moral universe, desire, like the speed of light for Einstein, is the *only* real absolute. But is this a "moral universe"? Can desire taken as an absolute acknowledge any limits? Where nothing is forbidden, nothing is sacred. And according to the consumerist view, nothing is sacred except personal and unlimited desire.

Experience and history suggest that unleashing unquenchable appetites leads inevitably to corruption and decay, personally and collectively. This outcome is both objectively clear and statistically proven. Beyond the statistics, it is true for deeper reasons. We become miserable under conditions of unlimited desire because we are created to live under a sacred canopy. Because this is who we are, we can see and gauge the loss of sacred meaning directly in our lives. Accepting moral limits is a key to our happiness because moral limits require us to accept challenges to our pride and complacency. This is part of what it means to take a sacred moral code seriously. The Jewish people were

God's chosen people, not because God let them do whatever they wanted. His Ten Commandments were conceived, not as a form of repression, nor as a denial of the core goodness of human desire, but as a call to self-sacrifice in the name of that which is most fully human.

I think we could do with more emphasis, especially in these opening pages, on thrift as a Biblical and humanist virtue. Admittedly, I will go on to cite the Parable of the Talents and broaden the picture by bringing in more from Aristotle and also Aquinas, but I wonder whether we couldn't mention these here. Too much Calvinism and Scottishness perhaps risks making the argument look narrow and culture-specific. The theme of plenitude and extravagance, the woman with the jar of nard (Mark 14:3), for example, is not to be forgotten. Here, blessings are pressed down and running over. There can never be enough on the subject of how thrift is not opposed to richness, lavishness, and prodigality but a necessary ingredient in the proper enjoyment of abundance, helping to offset the tendency that the word has to be a synonym for meanness, a Trojan Horse for niggardliness. Thrift stands on a sliding slope above parsimony and needs constantly to be working against that gravitational pull. I can't make this point too often. Thrift is *not* a mask for something negative. Thrift is *not* even something neutral. Thrift is positive, wise, prudential, intelligent, grateful, and always self-controlled.

Few modern illusions have riveted the imagination as overwhelmingly as the myth of the Hollywood-invented American Dream, with its emphasis on high consumption, compulsive acquisition, and instant gratification. In their book *Affluenza: The All-Consuming Epidemic,* authors John De Graff and Thomas Naylor describe a "painful, contagious, socially transmitted condition of overload, debt, anxiety, and waste resulting from the dogged pursuit of more."[2] This metaphor of a disease is a relevant characterization of a malignant condition eating into the heart of America. The insatiable urge to acquire things, whether or not they are needed, has reached epidemic proportions. This epidemic has caused severe social and cultural dislocations and warped the basic values of American society. One of the most corrosive impacts of this overheated consumerism is on human relationships. Flourishing in a throwaway culture, the attitudes formed in relation to products eventually get transferred to people as well. Just as things are discarded after casual use, people are cast off if they lose capacity to participate in the cycle of consumption or to gratify the easy appetites of their companions. In a consumerist culture, people too are consumed.

What remedy or alternative moral universe can be recommended as a counterforce to unbridled consumerism? Many have stated the problem and suggested the need for balance. What is the moral character of desire that is also complementary to capitalist economic activity? If we want an economy that produces abundance, is it not true that excess is an inevitable result, since we are flawed and never hit the mark perfectly and constantly? Do we not need to suggest some range that is acceptable? Or perhaps a golden mean for desire in developed economies?

Is there such a thing as enough? Can one overdevelop? Innately we know the answer to these perplexing questions, and the answer is moderation. And the virtue that guides moderation is —thrift.

## THE MORAL CHALLENGES OF UNDERDEVELOPMENT

Two thirds of the world does not have this problem, at least not to the degree we experience it in developed economies. In the vast majority of areas people strive simply to *survive*. This does not mean they do not consume or want to consume. It just means that they have not to date been able to consume at anything like the rate or scale experienced in the West.

It also does not mean that these non-consumerist societies exist in a state of moral beatitude. Some in the academic world and populist/socialist political leaders see undeveloped societies as superior to developed, consumerist societies. But the excesses of consumerism do not mean that poverty is the answer. In fact, lack of development has its own moral shortcoming.

Among the many moral concerns that confront us in the contemporary world, underdevelopment is perhaps as glaring a problem as overheated consumerism. One stark reality apparent at the beginning of this new millennium is that two thirds of the world's population can barely sustain their lives, while a third of the world enjoys more than enough and controls most of the world's wealth and power. This is not to say that the wealthy one third has taken away the wealth of the other two thirds but to say that only a third of the world's population currently has the capacity to develop and use resources to raise populations above subsistence.

These persons—the majority of the citizens in the so-called developed countries (DCs), and elites in the developing countries—are well fed, housed, and educated and live relatively long and healthy lives. The majority of persons, by contrast, are subsisting in a pre-industrial era. The economies they know are, by and large, based on either subsistence farming or the export of primary products. The standard of living of the so-called less-developed countries (LDCs) hovers perilously close to subsistence, or even extinction. Except for a small and prosperous elite, the populations of the LDCs are afflicted by myriad ills. Over the last 50 years a number of countries have graduated from the ranks of the less developed to those of the developed, demonstrating that such progress is possible, even for large populations. It is occurring today in China and India on an unprecedented scale, as millions move from poverty to the middle class.

Any concept of betterment or "development" is based on the hope that all third-world citizens can and will eventually attain an improved standard of life and capacity to develop. Beyond this statement little agreement exists about development. Standard indices of development abound, and they typically include such elements as per capita income, the poverty line, and ratios of energy consumption, railroads, telephones, TVs, schools, teachers, students, literacy, death rates, and so on.

Within a framework of an ethical economics based on normative principles, the standard of life should not be narrowly defined, as is sometimes the case in positive economics—for development also includes aspects of human well-being, or what economists call welfare, such as health and access to medical care, food, education, housing, employment, the environment, religious and cultural values, and the sustainability of each of these. As significant as any of the indices of development may be, they do not capture the *whole* sense of what it means to develop. Particularly today, when the global economy is driven more and more by human factors, such as creativity and innovation, economic development hinges on health, education, and culture. To develop implies a material consumption function, but that is not the sum total of development.

Most researchers have concluded that improvement in the standard of life is difficult to imagine in countries with environments dominated by rival tribal and agrarian elites that do not want change, lack the administrative capacity to stimulate, regulate, and coordinate activities, and are plagued by situations caused by both external and internal actors and by uncertainty about rewards. Researchers, however, do not agree on the proper strategies *for* development. There recently emerged broad general agreement on the basic goals underlying development. The United Nations initiated its Millennium Goals in the last few years. The eight Millennium Development Goals (MDGs) range from halving extreme poverty to halting the spread of HIV/AIDS and providing universal primary education by the target date of 2015, based on a blueprint agreed to by the world's countries and leading development institutions. The goals are attempting to galvanize unprecedented efforts to meet the needs of the world's poorest. Yet the question that remains is how? Will a doubling of official development assistance achieve the goals that are called for, or is a different, more entrepreneurial, results-based approach necessary?

Chapter II will unravel some of the theories and strategies that contribute to our understanding of economic development, but in so doing I shall begin to address the core question: How do we understand economic development from a normative perspective? I will discuss *four* main issues, to each of which a separate section is addressed. First, I will look at development shortcomings and then at successes of the last 50 some years. I conclude that while much has been accomplished, the job is still far from finished. The cup is half full. Next, I inspect in some detail three major models of development, which have emerged in both economic literature and practice. I find each of them lacking. Then, I introduce a concept of economic development that is informed by norms and virtues such as thrift and entrepreneurship. Finally, the concluding section contains some possible recommendations for the future.

## SHORTCOMINGS OF DEVELOPMENT STRATEGIES

Apart from a few but growing number of elite groups, LDCs are not approaching parity with the world's developed states. Even the most "optimistic" estimates of economic and technological measures suggest that the differences between rich and poor may even increase over the next decades due to the rate of technological advancement and income levels within developed countries. This is not to say that some countries have not made incredible progress in overcoming poverty. Nonetheless, some recent statistics (reported in a U.S. State Department study) reveal that currently there are:

- 1.2 billion people without sufficient access to water;

- 800 million people without enough to eat;

- 15 million children dying per year from malnutrition;

- 550 million people who cannot read or write; and,

- 220 million people without adequate shelter.

The level of economic development and the development process itself have been the subject of massive economic and social research over the last five decades. Here are some reasons that are often offered in answer to the question: "Why are the LDCs so poor?"

- they lack investment capital;

- they lack foreign markets for export goods;

- they are overdependent on one or two primary commodities;

- they maintain archaic and unproductive agrarian sectors with disincentives for local farmers;

- they lack accessible natural resources;

- they are overpopulated and have excessive birthrates;

- they lack skilled labor and technology;

- they have outdated equipment and skills;

- they maintain bureaucratic and often corrupt or mismanaged para-statal institutions; and,

- they have inadequate infrastructure and social institutions.

On the cultural side, other factors are said to be detrimental to development, which anthropologists claim are due to lingering traditional patterns. These would include such factors as:

- lack of entrepreneurship;

- weak family orientations;

- low savings;

- propensity to squander resources;

- fragmentation of land and wealth; and

- reluctance to think in terms of economies of scale.

However, according to World Bank and U.N. sources, for more than 50 years now an increasingly effective development effort has brought about an improvement in the human condition unprecedented in the annals of human history. Most parts of the world have overcome rampant disease and hunger. For much of humankind, illiteracy has been vanquished. This analysis defines resources broadly; resources include not only natural resources but also human resources such as mental, social, spiritual, and physical health.

From 1950 to 2004, the share of developing countries in world industrial output rose from 5 percent to 25 percent. Developing countries as a group increased their real gross domestic product fivefold, their industrial output tenfold, their gross capital formation almost twelvefold, their skill formation (based on the number of colleges and technical degrees awarded) sixteenfold. These figures should be considered in the light of rapid population growth.

Much of the credit for sustained accomplishments must go to the LDCs themselves. These countries have marshaled the overwhelming proportion of the human and material investment required for advancement. As the Nobel prize-winning economist Theodore Schultz put it, "The achievements of many low-income countries in their private and public investments in human capital are indeed impressive given their resource constraints."[3] Official development assistance has in many instances, though not uniformly, served as a catalyst in this development process.

Here are some compelling figures that give evidence of the massive efforts made by and on account of LDCs:

- About a third of adults (in developing countries) were literate in 1950. Now the proportion has advanced to nearly 60%.

- Life expectancy for LDCs as a group rose from 43 to 64 years during the same period.

- Child mortality declined from 28 per thousand children aged 1 to 4 years in 1950 to less than 10 per thousand by 2004.

- Skill formation has grown dramatically, especially in research and skilled manpower.

- Primary school enrollment increased sharply from 56% in 1960 to 78% in 1978 to over 88% today. Secondary schools showed an even greater increase.

- Enrollment in universities rose by more than 14% yearly to a current level 16 times that of 1950.

The cup may be half empty, but it is also half full. We should not forget the development successes when assessing real current needs. As a recent World Bank *World Development Report* said: "Human development offers the prospect that living standards can be improved even faster. This long term improvement in human beings is the one bright spot that is shared by almost all developing countries."[4]

## CONTENDING DEVELOPMENT STRATEGIES

Three major competing theoretical models, or strategies of development—"neo-classical," "neo-Marxist," and "structuralist"—have become prominent over the course of the last five decades. Each has, in its own way, affected development economics and the policies pursued by rich and poor alike. The early neo-classical or "modernization" models, rooted in the growth experiences of Western industrial nations, assumed that development occurred when nations progressed through "stages of growth"[5] beginning in a "traditional society" and arriving at the final stage of high-mass consumption. The history of South Korea, Taiwan, Hong Kong, and Singapore were cited as illustrations. Third-world nations, it was argued, can be expected to pass through these same stages, as technology, skills, and attitudes are transferred and transformed via development aid and, most important, foreign direct investment. The modernization model argued that the burden of change rests on the LDCs themselves. It emphasized innovation, the mobilization of domestic resources—including human resources, capital formation, and technical progress as the sources of economic growth. It also considered favorably the role of external finance and the need for liberalized and expanded trade. In agricultural programs it was assumed that peasants would adopt modern farming techniques when it was demonstrated that they would increase yields and income if followed. Focusing almost exclusively on economic growth, the neo-classical theories are widely accepted by professional Western economists, developed-country aid agencies, and the post-war international economic institutions such as the World Bank, IMF (International Monetary Fund), and WTO World Trade Organization They have, however, come in for criticism as overly governmental.[6] They have also been questioned from both left and right by traditionalists, religionists, and those less keen on Western business models and consumption.

The "dependency" perspective on development was developed from Marxist assumptions,[7] and maintained that the industrialized countries had enriched themselves at the

expense of third-world nations. This occurred first in colonial exploitation and later through capitalism and imperial-
ism, particularly through the vehicle of the transnational
corporation. According to various dependency theorists, ex-
ploitative relations have to be broken in order for true economic development to occur in third-world settings. Little
attention was focused on the internal dynamics for growth
in individual LDCs. Rather, the international capitalist system was castigated. All "dependency" theories are attempts
to vindicate the basic tenet of Marxist thinking in all its
forms, which is that if, in some economic relationship, one
party is rich and the other poor, then the wealth of the one
must be purchased by the poverty of the other. Economics
is a zero-sum game. This idea, which Marx attempted to
prove through his theory of exploitation and the wage contract, was definitively exploded by the Austrian economists
Hayek and von Mises. But its emotional appeal is sempiter-
nal, since it allows us to *blame* the rich for their possessions
and therefore to place a claim on them. Not surprisingly,
therefore, it is the kind of theory that is eagerly embraced
by the poor countries themselves.

The dependency theories took root in the fertile
ground of Latin America and then via the New International
Economic Order (NIEO) throughout the entire developing world. The resurgence of neo-classical development
economics in the late 1960s and 1970s from Solow, Kaldor,
Kahl, Inkeles, and Smith [8] coincided with a more radical
movement toward increased concern for unemployment,
poverty, and "basic needs." Although some of these thinkers
would place themselves outside the mainstream of develop-

ment thinking, such as Healey, Myrdal, and Singer, [9] they utilized dialectical logic to present capitalism as the sole cause of third-world economic stagnation. Underdeveloped "peripheral regions," with their cheap labor and raw materials, are, Flinn and Brown argued, drained by the developed "core" countries in Europe and North America.[10] They argued that diffusion of modern farm technology to large farmers causes prices of crops to drop due to increased supplies; land holdings to increase in size; and poorer farmers, who cannot adapt, to migrate to cities to look for unskilled wage labor. Havens maintained that foreign aid programs in agriculture increase inequalities between countries and among social classes within countries because of built-in biases "against the poor."[11]

"Structural" hypotheses about development were formulated[12] in the late 1960s and 1970s by numerous third-world economists. It was argued that general inflexibility applies to the poor countries and that production structures in developing countries are essentially different from those in developed countries. According to authors like Rodan, Lewis, Prebisch, Chenery, and Nurkse, in order to achieve development the structures in the third world need to approximate more closely those of the developed countries. While distrusting the price mechanism, the socialist-oriented structuralists tended to ignore the influence of prices. Interdisciplinary in focus, they offered more of a sociopolitical than a technical economic theory of the development process.

The structuralist position holds that the money supply is exogenous and that only changing the structure of the economy—through land reform, more import substitution to make the economy less dependent on foreign trade, educational advancement, and improved fiscal systems—is of any avail in the long run. An inelastic supply of exports, inelastic world demand, or both, is an essential assumption of the structuralist view. Import substitution is favored, as are overvalued currencies, import controls, rapid industrialization, and the discouragement of export-led growth.

Where is development economics today? More recent debates in development macroeconomics have revolved around debt management, the appropriate role of the price mechanism, free trade policy, and the effect of policies in the DCs on the LDCs. At the micro level, questions concerning choice of planning techniques and investment criteria[13] have continued into the new century. The debate centers on whether capital-intensive projects produce the most growth. Planning for growth[14] has contributed to the emphasis on central planning, prevalent in many circles from the mid-1970s into the early 1990s. With the fall of the Soviet empire, much of the Central Planned Economy model also collapsed. Central concerns of development economics today are whether para-statal organizations are more or less efficient than market mechanisms in running an economy and what role agriculture should play. Micro lending has proven itself to be an effective development mechanism especially suited for the poorest populations. Development economists, of whatever stripe, have tended to caricature agriculture as a means for industrialization rather than as an end in itself. Nonetheless, agriculture continues to be viewed as a critically important element in the development process. China and India are now looked on as examples of rapid development on a scalable basis, using market-oriented structures to achieve unprecedented economic growth.

Development remains a great challenge to the third world. How can a country achieve it without putting undue pressure on the environment, on the resources—human, social, spiritual, and capital—on which development is based? How can a nation make development sustainable? What is enough development, or the proper strategy for development? This is the dilemma: How can the third-world countries design for themselves, in an increasingly integrated global economy, a path that appreciates questions such as these? In order to deal with these challenges, we need a renewed vision of development. Such a vision is essential so that we can evaluate existing theories and models of development.

What is development, after all? It is not just a goal of rational actions in the economic, political, and social spheres. It is also, and very deeply, the focus of redemptive hopes and expectations. In an important sense, as Peter Berger reminds us in *Pyramids of Sacrifice*, development is also a "religious" category.[15] Even for those living at the most precarious margins of existence, development is more than a matter of improved material conditions, although that is included. It is also a redemptive transformation: a move from one state of being, and one state of society, to another state in which order and well-being become the common concern. And to understand how development is to proceed in the underdeveloped world today, we ought to look more openly and carefully at how it was achieved in places like Scotland in the seventeenth and eighteenth centuries. It was not achieved by aid, by capital transfers, by central planning, or by any of the government-funded and government-corrupted schemes that prevail in the world today. It was achieved by thrift, by the virtue that dictated the wise use of resources and the growth of a public-spirited way of disposing of them. And thrift had its roots in the belief that God had entrusted the world to our care, as a gift that we should use wisely and for the common good.

I don't think the fundamental problem has changed since those days. A realistic view of development must be founded now, as it was then, on an understanding that resources are entrusted to us. God calls each of us to preserve and develop resources, and holds us accountable for managing them. The call to care for creation is based on redeeming love. We are redeemed and enter a new covenant relationship; we become a new creation and laws are written on our hearts. When we know these laws more intimately, we can respond creatively, and in the spirit of the law, to a call. Creative obedience to moral imperatives—to God's laws, natural law, and the norms expressed in the virtues—in our economic activities is one of the primary ways we can gratefully acknowledge love, grow into a mature relationship with nature and its Creator, confess, and celebrate our redemption.

Economic development is a process through which we learn to care for the resources that sustain life. We learn to be more responsible stewards while we experience and participate in an eternal kingdom. Economic development then can be viewed as progressively demonstrating creative management of endowed resources by stewards who know their master. Thus, genuine economic development is guided by character and takes into account the preservation needs of human beings and their physical, mental, social, and cultural lives. When we care for the creation, we inevitably deplete stocks of non-renewable resources; the second law of thermodynamics implies that the stock of ordered matter itself becomes smaller over time. We are entrusted with the responsibility to weigh the value of what is created (or produced) against the cost of the possibly nonrenewable resources that are invested. When we perform these valuations, we are not merely subject to the natural laws of physics or economics; we are also subject to the moral laws, which govern the created order. Therefore, our economic choices and valuations can never be purely value-free; they are either responsible or irresponsible decisions in light of the norms laid down in creation and revealed to us over time. As stewards we either obey or disobey the guidelines of our creator and master. Economic development, viewed from a normative perspective, is then rooted in God's own normative character and His call to participate in the building of a city with all the resources that have been entrusted to us.

Followers of economic norms should question whether families, communities, and societies live out of hope for the future or out of fear and anxiety. Ethics has long forcefully taught that seeking what is right first should guide all our activities. Real prosperity results from obedience to the laws, which are established as norms for all peoples. Therefore, genuine "economic" stewardship starts from these norms and laws; it does not find its deepest meaning in one overriding goal, such as growth in GNP, technological progress, or some other measure of efficiency, important as these may be. Living a life, even an economic life, of virtue means making sacrifices and following norms.

What does this mean for an increasingly interdependent, affluent, and ecologically vulnerable world? National economies as well as generations are more closely linked over time and space than ever before in the history of the planet. Wealth and prosperity increasingly depend on economic and ecological relationships, which include future generations, other nations, and other regions. Decisions on the use of nonrenewable resources and the direction of technological development substantially affect the world that future generations will encounter. We as inhabitants of the developed countries buy more goods produced in the LDCs, our banks invest our savings there, many of our jobs depend on exports to and imports from these countries, and our economic policies have major consequences for industries in Asia, farmers in Africa, and workers in South America.

Whether we appreciate it or not, these emerging relationships give us a new form of responsibility for both future generations and LDCs, particularly for the poorest people inhabiting those countries. This argument has focused on our responsibility toward the LDCs, which have quite literally become our neighbors, given the increasing interdependence and connectedness of the globe today. As the Good Samaritan encountered the robbed man, so do we increasingly encounter the poor in the LDCs in our integrated global economic relationships.

Just as the ancient prophets warned the Israelites that they could not have a secure society without justice, today we need to warn our interdependent world that there can be no true prosperity when affluent consumerist parts of the world do not care enough about those who lack the most elementary resources. True thrift is opposed to a culture of consumption and urges us to be generous to those in need. We cannot witness the distress and poverty of the LDCs and simply turn back to our next bout of self-indulgence. Such an attitude is neither just nor prudent, ignoring the fact that wars, insurrection, and violence often stem from the resentments of people whose distress is being ignored. It is disturbing to observe that many nations choose to bear the heavy costs of arming themselves against perceived threats while being ever less willing to set aside resources to foster just relations within their own borders and with other nations, or to establish sustainable relations with the natural environment. I do not imply that the LDCs were not our neighbors before. In colonial times, the colonial powers encountered the poor. Indeed, some of the current problems in development can be viewed as a legacy of our forefathers. The security and prosperity of individual nations, however, is increasingly dependent on globally sustainable development—or what others have termed "global integrity." And this means looking on other nations, whatever their state of development, as within the sphere of our moral concern.

Increasing economic and ecological interdependence between people also challenges us to reflect on the significance of justice. We are encouraged to replace our "exclusive" thinking of other countries as enemies and competitors with "inclusive" thinking of other nations as part of the world community—a body embraced by common grace. Emerging international economic relations offer a new and unique opportunity to foster greater mutual understanding and cooperation. More cooperation, instead of increasing conflict and strife, is possible, however, only when economic relations are perceived as just by all the participants. All countries and regions need to feel some degree of joint responsibility for managing global, ecological, and economic resources.

To a certain extent, many individual countries have come to realize that their domestic societies cannot function properly when the distribution of resources is grossly unequal. Consequently, they have taken measures to correct major inequities while allowing for an abundance of individual incentives and differences. In the same way, a healthy and sustainable interdependent world economy depends on a just distribution of world resources that allows for entrepreneurship, cultural differences, size of population, and political experience. When international economic relations are not mutually enriching, the LDCs are often tempted to retreat from the world community and to engage in conflict or terror on the developed nations. No one wants the poor nations to leave the world community; however, we need to show care toward those in need, so "they may continue to live among you." The best form of care is not a hand-out leading to long-term dependence but, rather, as the proverb suggests, teaching people how to fish for themselves so that in time they can have enterprises that prosper and populations that flourish. In other words, we must encourage the LDCs in the habit of thrift, so as to use their own resources profitably.

## SOME RECOMMENDATIONS FOR THE FUTURE

The developed nations and many developing countries to-day support an international economic system in which prices play an important role in allocating resources. A market-based system has assisted, and can continue to assist, the development process. Such a system encourages and disciplines people to participate and serve in their various economies. At the same time, it decentralizes economic decisions while respecting the responsibility of people to perform their own valuations. All economic systems, however, are subject to the laws laid down in creation; they can function properly only when provided with the proper inputs. This section discusses some of these required inputs in more detail: a distribution of resources that is just; public policies that protect the neediest; valuations and actions of the participants that attempt to be obedient to norms; and processes of wealth generation.

Both multilateral organizations and private voluntary organizations can help to allocate resources to the LDCs through concessionary financing of projects that directly benefit the poor. The basic objective of development aid is not simply to transfer income to the LDCs so that they can meet the consumption levels of the DCs. Instead, aid should be seen against the background of the call to all people—including the poor—to loving relations, through family, culture, and the wider society. Development assistance, therefore, should focus on strengthening the productive resources in the developing societies, through education, healthcare, improved infrastructure, and, most important, entrepreneurship. In this way, people can be helped to assume more effective and normative control over their resources. Aid is counterproductive when it makes LDCs more dependent upon DCs, when it breeds corruption or inefficient, bloated state bureaucracies. We know from experience that aid may destroy indigenous cultures and ecosystems, may create excessive pollution, and, by bypassing the mediating structures of civil society, may amplify the power of the state and the ability of the kleptocrats to seize command of it. Aid deserves the name only when tempered by a real concern for the common people and a desire to arm them *morally* against the culture of consumption and waste.

DCs should also respect the responsibility of the LDCs to choose their own path of development. Multilateral agencies, donor governments, and well-intentioned private voluntary organizations cannot impose their own models and expect lasting results. Instead, the providers of development assistance must encourage the LDCs to make normative choices by living out good examples, by helping them to assess their situation, and by providing information on the likely consequences—especially for the poor and future generations—of given economic choices. Such an interaction between LDCs and DCs contributes to greater mutual understanding and a fruitful use of resources.

I now turn to the role of public policies in the development process. In recent years, it has become increasingly clear that the trade policies and macroeconomic policies of the developed countries can significantly affect the development prospects of the LDCs, regions, individual groups, or single countries. Starting from a perspective dominated by anxiety about their own level of consumption and the adequacy of their defenses, in the beginning of the 1980s the developed countries pursued policies of large public deficits (that is, low savings) and some degree of protectionism. The DCs did not sufficiently take into account the often-disastrous consequences of these policies for the LDCs. Because the developed countries absorbed most of the world savings, less capital was left to finance investments in the LDCs. In addition, the worldwide shortage of capital resulted in an unanticipated increase in real interest rates, which hit the indebted LDCs particularly hard. That picture has now reversed itself. The innovations of global capital markets have resulted in an abundance of available capital seeking the highest return on investment.

The DCs also attempted to prevent adjustment to their industrial structures by protecting certain industries that competed with the exports of poorer countries. Consequently, the latter lost considerable export earnings. It has been estimated that the export earnings lost by the LDCs as a consequence of trade barriers in the DCs against agricultural products alone exceed the official development aid of all the DCs. This example illustrates how the developed nations, when their citizens and politicians do not demonstrate care and act out of anxiety about their own needs, disobey the norms that should guide their economic policies. When they are confronted with the consequences of their irresponsible policies they then try to correct some of the damage, but often in inefficient and insufficient ways.

Recent experience shows beyond doubt that we should support policies that increase savings in the developed nations, and also the responsible use of resources everywhere. Thrift should guide our domestic policies. And it should be the first of our exports. This action would not only counter the destructive effects of the consumer culture but also free resources for strengthening the productive resources in the LDCs and retraining workers in the DCs who lose their jobs because of exports from the LDCs. It would be the necessary first step toward putting relations between the developed and the undeveloped world on an equal and mutually respectful footing.

From this perspective it is undeniable that many LDCs have pursued policies that have discouraged a responsible use of resources. To convey an image of progress, the poorest countries have often put short-range objectives ahead of long-range, sustainable development. Many third-world leaders prefer steel mills and heavy industry instead of projects and industry compatible with basic needs, resources, and skills. This mistake is one of the most glaring development facts of the past decades.

Other policies followed by LDCs have also provided price signals that did not reflect the needs of their citizens.

To illustrate, LDC governments often kept producer prices for agricultural products low. In the short run, the urban population, a politically powerful group, benefited. In the long run, however, productive resources shifted away from agricultural production, thereby contributing to the scarcity of food. In addition, in many LDCs exchange rates were kept at artificially high levels. These policies of overvalued exchange rates resulted in capital flight and the underdevelopment of export industries, and thus the loss of essential foreign exchange. The political leadership in the LDCs will contribute significantly to the development of their own people when they pursue policies that provide more appropriate price signals. In LDCs and DCs alike, policies that are based on narrowly defined short-term interests of politically or ethnically powerful groups, disregarding the norms of justice and stewardship, are not responsible and will ultimately turn out to be counterproductive.

Economists have a responsibility to confront policymakers and citizens in both DCs and LDCs with the need for normative thinking and their responsibility for future generations and the poor. Multilateral organizations should better coordinate national policies that protect the disadvantaged members of the world community—and that will eventually benefit the whole world.

During recent years, multilateral organizations have required policy changes from the LDCs in exchange for the provision of financing, while the DCs have at times pursued policies that hurt the LDCs. This asymmetrical treatment, whereby the multilateral institutions effected only required policy changes in the LDCs, has frustrated the political leaders in the LDCs and has somewhat reduced their willingness to cooperate. As the developed nations more fully acknowledge their responsibility for the disadvantaged in the LDCs and move toward policies that take the interests of the LDCs into account, multilateral organizations and sovereign governments of the DCs will be in a better position to ask the political leadership in the LDCs to change their policies as well. The LDCs should coordinate their policies with those of the DCs in order to guarantee that the poor indeed are offered improved conditions for genuine development. Development should be seen as a joint responsibility of both DCs and LDCs.

This joint responsibility also applies to the continuing debt crisis; not only are the LDCs accountable, but also the DCs, the banks, and the multilateral organizations. When all parties acknowledge their joint responsibility for the neediest in the LDCs, some form of debt relief should be considered for the LDCs committed to responsible future policies. The continuing debt crisis, however, is not the cause of a crisis in development; it is a judgment on and a symptom of irresponsible policies in both the LDCs and DCs. Future crises can be prevented only through the pursuit of normative economic policies that improve the very conditions for development—in other words, policies that place economic virtues such as thrift at the heart of the developmental process.

So conceived, the development process is primarily an internal transformation of local communities, as people begin to manage resources as accountable stewards. Owing to their small size, the limited costs of their operation, their people-to-people experience, as well as their relative immunity to the pressures of politics and patronage, private voluntary organizations are often in the best position to effect the required changes in attitudes, valuations, and choices. Many of these organizations are grassroots, lean, and effective; a majority of them have some faith-based orientation or motivation. Not all of them are equally qualified, so a ratings system based on transparency and effectiveness would be useful to all donors.

## THE PROBLEM OF POVERTY

The problem of poverty is complicated and multifaceted, and it requires multidimensional solutions. Gone are the days when governments and private philanthropies simply give money to the poor and imagine that the poverty will vanish. Today, poverty reduction planners focus on issues such as well-functioning legal and monetary institutions, rule of law, access to markets, transparency, and ample flows of capital. Increasingly, these planners are also beginning to realize that an essential ingredient of wealth creation is something intangible—what might be interpreted as a *spiritual outlook* in which hard work and determination are valued, and where individuals are energized by, react to, and proactively take advantage of the benefits of free competition. In this picture of evolving prosperity, the beneficiary is empowered and dignified instead of treated as "poor" and less than respectable.

Today the globally integrated economy is focused more than ever on the "impoverished market" or what some have dubbed "the Bottom of the Pyramid." The next big top-line growth opportunity is where you least expect to find it—the more than three billion people in the world that live on under $2 a day. Up to now, they have often been dismissed as too poor, too inaccessible, and too costly to serve in order to become profitable consumers. The reality is that rural to urban migration is making this population easier to reach, and they have more disposable income than might be apparent. The world's vast poor populations in Asia, Africa, the Middle East, and South America, predominantly, can also be a significant source of cost savings, new ideas, and talent. They are for the most part eager to learn and to work. Of course, companies need to be more creative and adaptive in seeking local brands and business partners, smaller package sizes, and low-cost distribution channels. Once, most Europeans and North Americans were themselves poor, and companies eventually found ways to market to them, using door-to-door salesmen for inexpensive life insurance, books, Bibles, and household and cosmetic supplies. These are lessons worth relearning and updating in the one really large untapped market still left.

However, all such initiatives should occur within a normative framework, one that respects the real goal of economic transactions, which is the creation of a sustainable and self-renewing economy in which people can enjoy their full share of resources, without need or hardship. Such an economy will come about, I have argued, only if the people of the LDCs are motivated, as the Scots were motivated by their Calvinist beliefs, so as to take charge of their resources in an attitude of stewardship, to avoid profligacy and waste, and to work together in a spirit of charity. In economics, as in every area of life, we are called to redemption, and the first step to redemption is the love of one's neighbor.

Taking such a call as an orientation point in economic life does not, however, offer some lock-step controls for a new world economic order. Rather, it offers normative guidelines that need to be tested, not in some perfect plan but from the ground up, for public policy and daily economic decisions. Persons and communities in both the DCs and the LDCs have to learn how to apply these normative guidelines in an increasingly interdependent world. It is our hope that other religions also hold some of the same or related normative guidelines. Whether sovereign nation states disappear or new regimes with international functions emerge is less important than the fact that inhabitants of the planet recognize their responsibility to wisely steward what has been entrusted to them. All of us, in whatever position we find ourselves—policymaker, economist, consumer, employer, employee—are called to be signs of a future, which includes all human concerns.

The full manifestation and fulfillment of any kingdom on earth will not be the result of our own activities alone. We cannot fully liberate the whole created order from its present bondage. In our economic lives, however, we should anticipate this future even as it is already here. Here and now, we must strive to be ambassadors for creation. Conservation is an ethic as well as a life choice, and thrift is a fundamental part of it. This idea leads us to ask what a blueprint based on a virtue-based value system might look like and what contribution would be expected of us as "reasoned agents" of change rather than "needy patients." I began by focusing on life in more developed countries because this is where the greatest challenges of overconsumption and profligacy exist. But taking the beam out of your own eye is never easy, because of fixed ways and ideas and because it soon gets personal. Normative values provide powerful and timely insights into stewardship responsibility, the integrity of creation, exploitation through self-interest and greed, love for our neighbors, and care for the needs of future generations.

Sir Brian Heap, the noted British scientist and international authority on subjects such as climate change and scientific exchange, has contributed to our thinking on these subjects and has shaped my argument here.[16] He argues that consumption increased immensely over the second half of the twentieth century, a period in which overall economic activity quintupled, energy use more than quadrupled, food production tripled, and world population more than doubled. Business-as-usual scenarios suggest a slowing of these rates over the next 50 years, although consumption rates are predicted to increase at well beyond the rate of population growth, and energy is anticipated to show a fivefold increase over the next 100 years.

Nowadays, more than a quarter of individuals worldwide live a lifestyle once limited to rich nations. This laudable improvement means that, while the average Chinese and Indian still consumes much less than the average North American or European, the combined consumption of India and China is larger than that of Western Europe. Heap has shown that in China 240 million people have been classified as "new consumers," and there will soon be more of them than the total number of consumers in the United States. At least one fifth of global car ownership is attributable to these new consumers, and by 2010 this figure could have risen to one third. The explosive rise of living standards in China is reflected by a 2.5-fold increase since 1994 in the ownership of color televisions (82% of households now own one), landline phones (63%), video players (50%), and mobile phones (at least one phone in 400 million households). Despite these statistics, the proportion of Chinese expressing satisfaction with the way things are in their lives has actually declined over time, mostly because of the ills associated with the urban environment compared with the lifestyle of the countryside—a telling example that consumption and economic prosperity have not delivered a "promised land" for its inhabitants. How does this scenario relate to the conventional sustainability paradigm necessary for long-term global survival and functioning, and how does if fit with the cherished values foundational to spiritual principles and attitudes?

Population growth is frequently perceived as a macrodriver of consumption and unsustainability, but the picture is not as straightforward as sometimes suggested. Heap asserts that Britain has a population growth of 0.1%, adding an extra 59,000 people each year to a population of 60 million. Bangladesh has a growth rate of 2.2%, producing an extra 3.2 million people per year to go with 147 million. Each new British consumer uses 45 times more fossil fuel than each new Bangladeshi, so the population growth in Britain produces almost as many $CO_2$ emissions as those from the 54 times larger population growth of Bangladesh.

In countries such as China, India, Brazil, Mexico, and Russia the combination of population growth and economic development is resulting in a class of new consumers that is likely to redraw the economic map of the world. In 2014 it is estimated that new consumers in these countries alone could well number over one billion and account for 20% of the world's purchasing power.

The urge to acquire must have been one of the innate drives that enabled the survival of our earliest ancestors. It differs today only to the extent that rational analysis plays a part in our choices. The dominant view of human behavior emerging from studies in evolutionary adaptation and psychology is that the adoption of a sustainable lifestyle is countercultural and will not come naturally. Our desire to acquire and consume is insatiable as well as immediate and inbuilt.

Consumer behavioral traits may offer selective advantages but at the same time be pathological and even irrational. Psychological denial may manifest itself as a failure to face up to health-threatening behavior, as in obese consumers, but even to an impending potential disaster. Pollsters assessing people's attitude about the possibility of a dam bursting high above where they lived found that concern fell to zero the nearer one approached the dam. In the present context, any proposal for change concerning consumption and production must not only contend with self-serving behavior and denial but also appeal to the importance of strengthening collectively those social and moral behaviors that influence consumption patterns and value the planet for both our own future happiness and that of future generations.

For most people, happiness is the main, if not the only, objective of life. David Myers, the social psychologist, demonstrated these sentiments in his well-researched book *The Pursuit of Happiness*.[17] He sees, however, that there are two senses in which happiness can represent a state of people's well-being. The traditional sense is of happiness as a one-dimensional hedonic expression of our feelings—a transitory and subtle representation of our self-satisfaction with life. The second sense is of happiness as an expression of a fulfilling life. In this sense happiness is achieved through our long-term goals and sense of autonomy in our daily affairs of life.

Attempts to measure what gives us the greatest happiness are not easy. Subjective happiness expressed in pleasant effects, such as elation, joy, contentment, and ecstasy, has been assessed by physiological and neurobiological indicators, by observing social and nonverbal behavior, and by questionnaires. In order of importance, the five most important factors are family relationships, financial situation, work, community and friends, and health. Personal freedom and personal values also play a major part; it is also claimed that happiness can be lastingly increased.

Individual perception of standard of living is regularly mentioned as one of the most important elements of happiness. Annual surveys of more than 20,000 students entering colleges in the U.S. show a growing proportion asserting that it was very important to be rich and a declining number saying that it was very important to develop a meaningful philosophy in life. Nonetheless, according to the National Opinion Research Center, the correlation in the U.S. between happiness and income is only 0.2, while in Switzerland the highest-income recipients report a lower sense of well-being than does the income group immediately below.

Clearly, there are many reasons why high income and material prosperity do not simply translate into greater happiness. Aggregated indicators of material well-being say very little about how higher-income levels are distributed among different individuals and social groups. It is logically possible that income per capita grows with higher-income concentration: People compare themselves with others, and their relative income is what becomes important. Moreover, aspiration levels adjust to the rise in income (the "hedonic treadmill effect"); people get used to the higher-income level, which then produces less happiness for them than what they would enjoy if no such adjustment had taken place. Lottery winners are very happy after winning, but their happiness levels revert near the original level after some weeks. The clear conclusion from Myers's and other happiness research is that the relationship between happiness and per capita income is not close, although it is well established that people in rich countries are generally happier than those in poor countries.

We can summarize the argument so far: Consumption, though necessary for human welfare, is not a sufficient requirement for happiness, while prosperity gained at the expense of the habitability of the planet is perverse. If unsustainable consumption has such a low impact on individuals' well-being, is there an alternative based on normative values? If so, what part might thrift have to play in it?

The modern dilemma is that the desire for happiness is not guaranteed by an obsession with economic growth and unbridled consumption. This situation provides an opportunity to consider a more hopeful alternative. As long ago as 1795 the French mathematician and Enlightenment thinker Condorcet expressed the hope that people might reason their way into achieving technical progress as well as behavioral adjustments. He wrote that "a very small amount of ground will be able to produce a great quantity of supplies of greater utility or higher quality; more goods will be obtained from a smaller outlay; the manufacture of articles will be achieved with less wastage in raw materials and will make better use of them".[18] Condorcet had the prescience to anticipate the importance of sustainable consumption and production in a century when life was very different. However, neither Condorcet nor Malthus (1798) foresaw the remarkable impact of scientific and technological advances, which would arrest the occurrence of widespread global famine.

Sustainable consumption lies at the heart of the concept of sustainable development. It enriches our understanding of sustainable development because it emphasizes the need for consumption habits and attitudes to change. The practical objectives of sustainable consumption and production are broad:

- to reduce the consumption of natural resources by improvements in the efficiency of processes and services;

- to minimize the emissions of waste, pollutants, and toxic materials over the life cycle of products, processes, and services;

- to create new materials with long life, durability, and reusable properties;

- to conserve biodiversity for current needs and freedoms; and

- to address disparities between more- and less-developed countries and protect the needs of future generations.

The extent of these objectives means that a compromise is almost unavoidable between the technological and the ethical dimensions of economic decisions if a definition of sustainable consumption and production is to carry enough consensuses for practical purposes.

Consumption is widely perceived as an expression of a prosperous society. What are the expressions of a thrifty or frugal society? Consumption helps to win votes at election time. Whether consumption as our sole priority can be taken to be good for us is another matter. We may see it as synonymous with improved well-being so that the more we consume the better off we are, or we may regard it as environmentally and psychologically threatening to our quality of life. Arguments for any change in attitude will have to be accessible as well as persuasive.

Traditional economic measures, such as the gross national product (GNP) used by most governments, also can lead to flawed decisions. GNP is deeply engrained in political life as an assessment of a nation's economic progress and standing. However, a nation's capital assets can take several forms; they require measures of the net changes in manufactured and human capital, public knowledge, and natural capital. As an indicator GNP is insensitive to the depreciation of capital assets and does not recognize the net value of changes in externalities such as the environment-resource base.[19] As a result, consumers are confused about true costs. If wealth and social well-being are taken as equivalent, it is possible that GNP can increase for a time even while the country becomes poorer and social well-being declines. The moral is banal: GNP is not necessarily a measure of the quality of life. If we were to get used to the term net national product (NNP), which has been proposed as an alternative, it would represent a more realistic assessment of sustainable development by taking account of and internalizing environmental costs. It would also begin to restore older notions of thrift and savings.

## CHAPTER THREE

# Virtue and the Moral Life

*"He who does not economize will have to agonize."*
—Confucius

The previous chapter explored an area in which economic virtue, though very much needed, is seldom invoked, with serious results for the new world economy. I suggested that thrift is as much needed by the developing countries today as by the developing countries of Europe in the seventeenth century. But more needs to be said about the nature of virtue in general and what it brings to human individuals and the communities to which they belong.

Philosophers have long argued for a connection between virtue and happiness. For the Greeks happiness consisted in an order of the soul, expressed in the Delphic mottos "know yourself" and "nothing to excess." Aristotle expanded these moral hints into a complete moral philosophy—perhaps the most persuasive that has ever been devised, and one that, through the writings of St. Thomas Aquinas, was to become fundamental to the Christian worldview.

Aristotle thought that habits of doing right always looked at the *median* as the best course. He considered both the deficiencies and the excesses as vices to be avoided. His advice in essence was to lean toward that extreme toward which one is least prone.[1] In thrift, that would mean the ideal is to be generous—avoiding on the one hand cheapness and on the other extravagance.

The mean is a generous life. This implies that a person of thrift does not exclude generosity but rather encompasses it. John Templeton, Jr., M.D., has written eloquently about combining the two qualities in *Thrift and Generosity: The Joy of Giving*.[2] He recommends, "Thrift is not so much a matter of how much we have, but of how we appreciate, value, and use what we have. Everyone, regardless of income level, has opportunities to exercise the virtue of thrift. We practice thrift by monitoring how we spend our time and money and then by making better decisions."[3]

The parable Jesus told of the talents illustrates the point. Recall that it begins with a wealthy man going on a long journey who chooses three servants to look after his resources, or talents (currencies) in his absence. While he is gone each will be judged on proper behavior. He gives the first servant five talents, the second two talents, and the last only one talent. While he is gone, the first servant puts his master's talents to immediate work. In fact, when the master returns, the servant has turned the five talents into ten. The second servant was as successful turning two talents to four. The master is most pleased with the results of such thrift and stewardship. The two servants showed themselves true stewards of the assets entrusted to them. The final servant, who was guided not by stewardship but by fear and lethargy, does not please him. The third servant did nothing with the talent. He simply dug a hole in the ground and buried it for safekeeping. The master punished him by taking the only talent entrusted to him and giving it to the servant who had ten talents. The *moral* of the parable is shockingly clear: Focus on what you have been given and make creative use of it. It points unquestioningly to hard work and industry, to the wise use and investment of all resources, and to the moral value of risk-taking.

If thrift were a form of stinginess, the third servant would have demonstrated real thrift. The third servant took the maximum precaution to hold on to what he had, to be sure that what he possessed was neither diminished nor lost. Such management is inspired by fear and manifests the highest levels of control. Instead of praising such behavior, the parable shows that it is in fact a false thrift. Virtuous stewardship includes risk-taking, personal responsibility, and vision. It is generous, both in its outlook toward the future and in its expectation for effort, and bountiful in its results.

Thrift in this famous and often quoted passage is not just a better, "stricter" reading of the bottom line. As Jack Templeton says, "Rather, it is part of a spiritual and cultural understanding of how we are to use our time, our talents, and our resources. Creating a culture of thrift means embedding this virtue in a larger framework of personal responsibility, discipline, purpose, and future-mindedness."[4] This attitude is perhaps best summarized in the words of the founder of Methodism, John Wesley, when he said, "Make all you can; save all you can; give all you can."[5]

In the *Merchant of Venice* Shakespeare addresses the great question of how to integrate the life of commerce with the demands of morality. Thrift is central to the drama, and in the character of Shylock Shakespeare paints one of the vices with which true thrift is to be contrasted—the vice of meanness. And he shows how this vice is not manifest in the monetary sphere only, but infects the whole character with a kind of vindictive solipsism. True thrift is embodied in the character of Antonio, who lives the life of a hard-working merchant, a generous friend and patron, and a risk-taker who is capable of undertaking large-scale projects for his own and others' good.

Shylock's meanness also exemplifies the strict legalism that accompanies such an outlook toward money. Placing this vice at the center of his moral universe, Shylock taints and distorts the whole range of his character and behavior and puts vice in place of virtue in all the places where the two compete. Thus, the higher virtue of justice becomes twisted by Shylock's miserliness into a bloodless legalism, if the pun may be permitted. For Shylock, thrift is ungenerous and justice unforgiving, so that true thrift and true justice are alike foreign to his nature. Neither mercy nor generosity can take root in his heart, and the result is a wasted life and the loss of all he possessed, as happened to the third servant in Christ's parable.

Shylock's miserliness shines through in large ways in the major action of the plot and also permeates the daily details of his life. For example, in a pivotal scene, he tells his daughter three times to "lock the doors"—this in the hour that she will rob his house and abscond with a Christian—"Fast bind, fast find— a proverb never stales in thrifty mind." The word "thrift" is used seven times in the play, five of them as commendation in the modern sense, always in Shylock's mouth, framed by two uses in a different sense by other characters. Shylock discovers that a life based on ultimate control and hoarding—in other words, on one of the vices that ensue when thrift is pried free of the virtues—is self-destructive. Perhaps we should also mention Hamlet on thrift as well as Shylock. "Thrift, thrift, Horatio! The funeral baked meats did coldly furnish forth the marriage tables!" Hamlet's tone suggests that, even in Elizabethan England, thrift could sometimes be seen as a euphemism for something morally questionable.

We are not arguing that thrift can take the central place in the constellation of virtues, much less that thrift, misunderstood as "miserliness," leads to the virtuous life. Quite the opposite: The position here is that true thrift has to be understood as the golden mean of generosity and that it must be integrated into a full range of virtues in a balanced, well-integrated life. Thrift in conjunction with the other virtues in a sound and complete orbit leads to the good life. Likewise, the other virtues practiced without a sense of thrift and its twin, temperance, can easily fall short and even be overcome in excess, acquisitiveness, and the sheer accumulation of things to no end.

The root of *thrift* is the verb (of Old Norse origin) "to thrive." The thrifty person, as a thriving person, has a reasonable concern with both the present and the future. Thriftiness is not stinginess. Thrifty persons show a respect for both their own and others' future and financial stability. They are very mindful of the needs of others. They neither hoard nor engage in conspicuous consumption. They do not buy in excess, but they do plan for their financial future. Theologically, saving is not only a part of salvation; it is also worked out in redemptive works of sanctification.

The major virtues in the Western tradition are the four pagan virtues of courage, justice, temperance, and prudence and the three theological virtues of faith, hope, and charity, or love. Four plus three equals the Seven Virtues, a combination most thoroughly analyzed by St. Thomas Aquinas: the four virtues of the polis and the three virtues of the monastery. It is not absurd to connect the four pagan virtues with Socrates and the three theological virtues with Jesus—the two great models on which our tradition of moral excellence has been based, the one epitomizing Athens and the other Jerusalem. Charismatic figures, both men were masters who left no written teachings and founded no schools but who simply set an example. In the efforts of their disciples, in the passionate narratives inspired by their deaths, we see the beginnings of the inward vocabulary, the encoded recognitions of our entire moral, philosophical, and theological idiom.

In many ways discipleship became, through these two great examples, fundamental to Western morality. The charged personal encounter between *master* and *disciple* has also interested the classicist George Steiner in his many books, most notably *Lessons of the Masters*, a sustained reflection on the infinitely complex and subtle interplay of power, trust, and passions in the most profound sorts of pedagogy.[6] Steiner considers a diverse array of traditions and disciples, returning throughout to three underlying themes—the master's power to exploit his student's dependence and vulnerability; the complementary threat of subversion and betrayal of the mentor by his pupil; and the reciprocal exchange of trust and love, of learning and instruction, between teacher and disciple. Can we relearn what has been lost or forgotten?

Virtue and the moral life must be founded on something; they are always grounded. They are not relative or subjective, as we have come to think of most preferences in the last two centuries. For thousands of years and in many different religious and philosophical traditions, some concept of transcendence has been the fulcrum for the development of virtues that in these past eras sustained human flourishing. Can it do so again? If you visit the great cathedrals in Europe, you would be convinced of a higher purpose as you stared at the arches leaping into the heavens and took in the liturgies and artwork of faith. I have been to many of these places and in almost all have seen some profound visual depiction of virtue. They typically follow an iconographic program inspired by the prevailing Scholastic thought, with reliefs representing the human activities related to the virtues of *necessitas* (civil life, supreme sciences, intellectual speculation); the mythical inventions of the arts (painting, sculpture, and architecture); liberal arts, grammar, dialectic, rhetoric, and arithmetic, medicine, geometry, and astronomy; the divine virtues (faith, hope, and charity); and the cardinal virtues (wisdom, justice, temperance, and courage). We need to reestablish a discussion on all these and modern virtues to recover what has been lost and to shine a light that could illumine our future.

Virtue ethics is a field that was dormant for centuries but is now coming back to life. Traditionally it has emphasized character over rules or consequences as the key element or driver of ethical thinking. In the West virtue ethics was the prevailing approach to ethical thinking in the ancient and medieval periods. The tradition suffered a complete eclipse during the early modern period as Aristotelianism fell out of favor. Virtue ethics returned to some prominence in philosophical thought during the twentieth century, and is one of three dominant approaches to normative ethics, the other two being deontology (the study of obligation and duty) and consequentialism (the theory that moral thinking is entirely about the costs and benefits of our actions).

Although concern for virtue appears in several different philosophical traditions, from the Chinese to other Eastern examples, in the West the roots of the tradition lie in the work of Plato and Aristotle. The tradition's key concepts derive from ancient Greek philosophy. These concepts include *arête* (excellence), phronesis (practical or moral wisdom), and eudaimonia (flourishing, sometimes translated as happiness). The term itself, "virtue ethics," is actually a relatively recent one. It has come to be something of an umbrella term that encompasses a number of different theories. Initially, virtue ethics was characterized as a movement focusing on the central role of character and virtue (which means "moral excellence" in Latin) in moral philosophy. Most virtue ethics theories still take their inspiration from Aristotle, although some versions incorporate elements from Plato, Aquinas, Hume, and Nietzsche. Virtue ethics originally defined itself by calling for a change from the dominant normative theories of deontology and consequentialism and headed down another, older path.

The ideas and books of the Notre Dame philosopher Alistair MacIntyre, particularly his classic *After Virtue*, are often cited as a stimulus for the increased interest in virtue.[7] MacIntyre's project is deeply critical of many of the notions, such as *ought,* which had been put in question by earlier virtue ethicists such as G.E.M. Anscombe and Bernard Williams.[8] However, he also attempted to give a full account of virtue. MacIntyre looks at a large number of historical accounts that differ in their lists of the virtues and have incompatible theories of the virtues. He concludes that these differences are attributable to different practices. Each account of virtue requires a prior account of social and moral features in order to be understood. Thus, in order to understand Homeric virtue you need to look at its social role in Greek society. Virtues, then, are exercised within practices that are coherent, social forms of activity and seek to realize goods internal to the activity. The virtues enable us to achieve these goods. There is an end, or *telos,* that transcends all particular practices, and it constitutes the good of a whole human life. That end is entailed in the virtue of integrity or constancy.

Recent virtue ethics writers have all, in their own way, argued for a radical change in the way we think about morality. Whether they call for a change of emphasis from obligation, a return to a broad understanding of ethics, or a unifying tradition of practices that generate virtues, their dissatisfaction with the state of modern moral philosophy suggests a need for the foundation of change.

Where deontology and consequentialism concern themselves with the right action, virtue ethics is concerned with the good life and what kinds of persons we should be. "What is the right action?" is a significantly different question from "How should I live?" or "What kind of person should I be?" Where the first type of question deals with specific dilemmas, the two others are questions about an entire life. Instead of asking what the right act is here and now, virtue ethics asks what kind of person one should be in order to get closer to right behavior all the time. Whereas deontology and consequentialism are based on (strict) rules that try to give us the right action, virtue ethics makes central use of the concept of character. The answer to "How should one live?" is that one should live virtuously, i.e., have a virtuous character.

Character and virtue are therefore forever joined in virtue ethics. In Aristotelian understanding, character is about a *state of being*. It is about having the appropriate inner states. For example, the virtue of kindness involves the right sort of emotions and inner states with respect to our feelings toward others. Character is also about doing. This means taking informed actions that are right. Aristotelian theory is a theory of action, since having the virtuous inner dispositions also involves being moved to act in accordance with them. The Latin and Greek roots for the term "virtue" involve power and the ability to act. Virtue, thus, is not a matter of following a set of external rules precisely and mechanically but of having an internal power or capacity to act in ways that exemplify some excellence. Thus, we come to understand what the virtue of social grace is by seeing a person who possesses the inner capacity to be graceful actually acting in a graceful manner. This action can never be reduced to a set of prescriptive rules, because the situations requiring grace and the capacity to be graceful are infinitely varied. The capacity is defined by real actions, but actions never define the capacity fully.

Character traits are stable, fixed, and reliable dispositions. If an agent possesses the character trait of kindness, we would expect him or her to act kindly in all sorts of situations, toward all kinds of people and over a long period of time, even when it is difficult to do so. A person with a certain character can be relied upon to act consistently over time. Moral character itself develops over a long period of time. People are born with all sorts of natural tendencies. Some of these natural tendencies will be positive, such as a placid and friendly nature, while others will be negative, such as an irascible and jealous nature. These natural tendencies can be encouraged and developed or discouraged and thwarted by the influences one is exposed to when growing up. There are a number of factors that may affect one's character development, such as one's parents, teachers, peer group, role models, the degree of encouragement and attention one receives, and exposure to different situations. Our natural tendencies, the raw material we are born with, are shaped and developed through a long and gradual process of education and habituation. This is a disciplined work of practice and contemplation over a lifetime, not a quick fix or something gained in a fell swoop or fast conversion.

Moral education and development is a major part of virtue ethics. Moral development, at least in its early stages, relies on the availability of good role models. The virtuous agent acts as a role model, and the student of virtue emulates his or her example. Initially this is a process of habituating oneself in right action. Aristotle advises us to perform just acts because in doing so we become just. The student of virtue must develop the right habits, so that they tend to perform virtuous acts. Virtue is not itself a habit, although it is constant, like a habit. Habituation is merely a means to the development of virtue, but true virtue requires choice, understanding, and knowledge. At the same time, as Aristotle taught, the moral virtues develop into such deeply engrained capacities that they operate without the need for conscious reflection. The kind person does not have to deliberate over whether or not to be kind, and indeed, real-life situations typically allow no such time for reflection. Virtuous action is prompt and done immediately. Later, the qualities of such action can be reflected upon, discussed, and refined in thought. But a virtuous person cannot engage rational decision-making in every action without losing the quality of real virtue. In this sense, virtue is habitual. The virtuous agent does not simply act justly out of an unreflective response but has come to recognize virtue in the actions of others and himself and why it is the appropriate response. Moral philosophy and great art, especially literature, help to develop this reflection on virtue. Virtue is chosen knowingly for its own sake. It is also performed without the effort of conscious thought or decision. The development of moral character takes a whole lifetime. But once it is firmly established, one will act consistently, predictably, and appropriately in a variety of situations.

Aristotelian virtue is defined in Book II of the *Nicomachean Ethics* as a purposive disposition, in the mean and being determined by the right reason. Virtue here is a settled disposition. It is also a purposive disposition. A virtuous person chooses virtuous action knowingly and for its own sake. It is not enough to act kindly by accident, unthinkingly, or because everyone else is doing so; you must act kindly because you recognize that this is the right way to behave. Although habituation is a tool for character development, it is not equivalent to virtue; virtue always requires conscious choice and affirmation along the way.

Virtue "lies in a mean" because the right response to each situation is neither too much nor too little. Virtue is the appropriate response to different situations and different agents. The virtues are associated with feelings or judgment. For example: Courage is associated with fear, modesty associated with the feeling of shame, and friendliness associated with feelings about social conduct. The virtue lies in a mean because it involves displaying the mean amount of emotion, where mean stands for appropriate. The mean amount is neither too much nor too little and is sensitive to the requirements of the person and the situation. Perhaps today the term "optimal" would be better than "mean," because we often think of the mean as a lifeless middle way—a form of meritocracy—whereas the golden mean is the optimal or most beautiful choice and action possible. And, indeed, one meaning of "mean" is "stingy," which is just what thriftiness ought *not* to be associated with.

Virtue is determined by right reason. Virtue requires both the right desire and the right reason. To act from the wrong reason is not to act virtuously. On the other hand, the agent can try to act from the right reason but fail because he or she has the wrong desire. The virtuous agent acts effortlessly, perceives the right reason, has the harmonious right desire, and has an inner state of virtue that flows smoothly into action. The virtuous agent acts as an exemplar to others.

These ideas about virtue are developed in great detail in Aristotle's works. I relate them here, as they have been central to virtue ethics' claim to put forward a unique and rival account to other normative theories. The emphasis on character development and the role of the emotions allow virtue ethics to have a plausible account of both moral psychology—which is lacking in deontology and consequentialism—and reasoned action. By displacing the problematic concepts of duty and obligation from the central position in ethics, in favor of the rich concept of virtue, we ensure that ethics is concerned with the whole life rather than with one isolated or situational action or incident.

In the first book of the *Nicomachean Ethics*, Aristotle warns that the study of ethics is imprecise. Virtue ethicists have challenged consequentialist and deontological theories because they fail to accommodate this insight. Both deontological and consequentialist theories rely on one rule or principle that is expected to apply to *all* situations. Because their principles are inflexible, they cannot accommodate the complexity of all the moral situations we are likely to encounter.

People are constantly faced with moral problems. Should I tell my friend the truth about her lying friend? Should I cheat in my examination to get ahead? Should I have an abortion? Should I risk my safety to save the drowning baby? Should we separate the Siamese twins? Should I join the protests? All these problems are different, and it seems unlikely that we will find the solution to all of them by applying the same rule. If the problems are varied, we should not expect to find their solution in one rigid rule that does not admit exception. If the nature of the thing we are studying is diverse and changing, then the answer cannot be any good if it is inflexible and unyielding. The answer to "How should I live?" cannot be found in one simple rule. At best, for virtue ethics, there can be rules of thumb— rules that are true for the most part but may not always be the appropriate response.

The doctrine of the mean captures exactly this idea. The virtuous response cannot be captured in a rule or principle that an agent can learn and then apply virtuously. As Plato said in the *Republic,* "It is not necessary to legislate to gentlemen." Knowing virtue is a matter of experience, sensitivity, ability to perceive, ability to reason practically, and this knowledge takes a long time to develop. The idea that ethics cannot be captured in one rule or principle is the "uncodifiability of ethics thesis." To put the rules model of ethics on its head, we might say that ethical rules are what virtuous persons would simply do without having to be told to do so. Ethics is too diverse and imprecise to be captured in a rigid code, so we must approach morality with a theory that is as flexible and as responsive as the subject matter itself. As a result, some virtue ethicists see themselves as anti-theorists, rejecting theories that systematically attempt to capture and organize all matters of practical or ethical importance.

Virtue ethics initially emerged as a rival of deontology and consequentialism in the early twentieth century. It developed from dissatisfaction with the notions of (Kantian) duty and obligation and their central roles in understanding morality. It also grew out of an objection to the use of rigid moral rules and principles and their application to diverse and different moral situations. Characteristically, virtue ethics has made a claim about the central role of virtue and character in its understanding of moral life and uses it to answer the questions "How should I live? What kind of person should I be?" Consequentialist theories are outcome-based and Kantian theories are agent-based. Virtue ethics, by contrast, is character-based.

Raising objections to other normative theories and defining itself in opposition to the claims of others characterized the first stage of the development of virtue ethics. Virtue ethicists then took up the challenge of developing full-fledged accounts of virtue that could stand on their own merits rather than simply criticize consequentialism and deontology. There are three main strands of development for virtue ethics—eudaimonism, agent-based theories, and the ethics of care.

*Eudaimonia* is an Aristotelian term loosely translated as happiness. Aristotle recognizes that actions have an aim: every action aims at some good. For example, the doctor's vaccination of the baby aims at the baby's health. Furthermore, some things are done for their own sake; they are ends in themselves. Some things are done for the sake of other things; they are means to other ends. Aristotle claims that all the things that are ends in themselves also contribute to a wider end, an end that is the greatest good of all. That good is eudaimonia. Eudaimonia is happiness, contentment, and fulfillment; it is the name of the best kind of life, which is an end in itself. It is a life, which includes "thrift" in the sense of thriving and living a flourishing life.

Aristotle then observes that where a thing has a function, the good of the thing consists in performing that function well. The knife has a function, to cut, and the good knife is one that cuts well. This argument is applied to man: Man has a function, and the good man is the man who performs his function well. Man's function is what is peculiar to him and sets him aside from other beings—reason. Therefore, the function of man is reason and the life that is distinctive of humans is the life in accordance with that reason. The good man is the one who lives so as to fulfill the demands of reason. Eudaimonia is the life of virtue—activity in accordance with reason, man's highest function.

The importance of this point, unique to eudaimonistic virtue ethics, is that it reverses the relationship between virtue and rightness. A utilitarian could accept the value of kindness, but only because someone with a kind disposition is likely to bring about consequences that will maximize utility. So the virtue is justified only because of the consequences it brings about. In eudaimonist virtue ethics the virtues are justified because they are constitutive elements of eudaimonia, i.e., human flourishing and well-being, which are good in and of themselves.

For this school of thinking the virtues themselves make their possessor a good human being. All living things can be evaluated *qua* specimens of their natural kind. The characteristic way of human beings is the rational way: by their very nature human beings act rationally, a characteristic that allows us to make decisions and effect change in our character and allows others to hold us responsible for those decisions and changes. One might think that the demands of morality conflict with our self-interest, as morality is other-regarding. However, eudaimonist virtue ethics presents a different picture. Human nature is such that virtue is not exercised in opposition to self-interest but rather is the quintessential component of human flourishing. The good life for humans is the life of virtue, and therefore it is in our own interest to be virtuous. It is not just that the virtues lead to the good life, where, if you are good, you will be rewarded. Rather a virtuous life is the good life because the exercise of our rational capacities in virtue is its own reward.

Not all accounts of virtue ethics are eudaimonist. Some philosophers have developed an account of virtue based on our common-sense intuitions about which character traits are admirable. They make a distinction between agent-focused and agent-based theories. Agent-focused theories understand the moral life in terms of what it is to be a virtuous individual, where the virtues are inner dispositions. Aristotelian theory is an example of an agent-focused theory. By contrast, agent-based theories are more radical in that their evaluation of actions is dependent on ethical judgments about the inner life of the agents who perform those actions. There are a variety of human traits that we find admirable, such as benevolence, kindness, compassion, or thrift, and we can identify these by looking at the people we admire, our moral exemplars.

ENCOUNTER BOOKS

900 Broadway

New York, New York 10003-1239

**www.encounterbooks.com**

**Please add me to your mailing list.**

Name

Company

Address

City, State, Zip

E-mail

Book Title

A third influential version of virtue ethics is the ethics of care. Developed mainly by feminist writers, this account of virtue ethics is motivated by the thought that men think in masculine terms, such as justice and autonomy, whereas woman think in feminine terms, such as caring. These theorists call for a change in the way we view morality and the virtues, shifting toward virtues exemplified by women, such as taking care of others, patience, the ability to nurture, self-sacrifice, and giving. These virtues have been marginalized because society has not adequately valued the contributions of women, it is argued.

There are other forms of virtue ethics, but the three types discussed here are representative of the landscape. Historically, of course, accounts of virtue have varied widely. There are many lists of virtues handed down through the ages, many of which are different or overlap significantly. Homeric virtue should be understood in the context of the society in which it occurred, where a man's worth was comparative to that of others and competition was crucial in determining it. Very different are the accounts of virtue ethics inspired by Christian writers such as Aquinas and Augustine. Aquinas's account allows a role for the will, which operates within the constraints of natural law. To possess a virtue is to have the will to apply it and the knowledge of how to do so. Humans are susceptible to evil, and acknowledging this allows us to be receptive to the virtues of faith, hope, and charity, virtues that are not mentioned by Aristotle.

The three types of theories, developed over long periods, answered many questions and often changed in response to criticism. Some have moved away from agent-based virtue ethics to a more Hume-inspired sentimentalist account of virtue. Hume-inspired accounts of virtue ethics rely on the motive of benevolence and the idea that actions should be evaluated by the sentiments they express. Others articulate admirable sentiments; still others express a concern for humanity. In all its many forms, however, virtue ethics is alive and well. There is increasingly a sustained and principled discussion in philosophical as well as practical circles about virtue and its effect on ethics and morality and everything it touches.

Recent advances in the social sciences also point to character traits or dispositions that equip people for greater success in the interpersonal world. These traits, which philosophers have called "virtues," include trust, generosity, faith, empathy, kindness, gratitude, forgiveness, and honesty, among others. Such traits are presumed to help people live lives in which they are useful to other people, seek just solutions to social dilemmas, and care for the welfare of others. Stephen G. Post and his Institute have researched and written about the ways these other-regarding virtues may also foster physical health or psychological and relational well-being. His book *Why Good Things Happen to Good People* is an up-to-date summary of the exciting new scientific research that proves the link between doing good and living a longer, healthier, and happier life.[9] Collectively strengthening the "other-regarding virtues" sheds light on how such virtues can be facilitated in laboratory and applied settings and also how they influence physical health, psychological well-being, and interpersonal relations.

Another recent opus published under the auspices of the American Psychological Association, edited by Christopher Peterson and Martin E. P. Seligman, *Character Strengths and Virtues: A Handbook and Classification*, lends yet more empirical support to the seven virtues and to character building.[10] In a lengthy treatment, using 2,300 citations to the technical literature in clinical and social psychology and related fields, the 40 drafters of the chapters (which Peterson and Seligman then rewrote) present a "manual of the sanities," that is, the "positive psychology" of healthy people. These are not mere assertions but findings, summarizing an extensive scientific literature.

Today we see where the philosophical, economic, psychological, and medical evidence, not just theories but conclusive scientific findings, all concur: A virtuous life is beneficial to the individual, to others, and to the economy and society in which one lives. Perhaps on such sound footing we should attempt to rediscover thrift, along with all the other virtues.

## CHAPTER FOUR

# The Consequences of Modern Selfishness

*"Cannot people realize how large an income is thrift?"*
—Cicero

It has been said you know a culture by its sins. In James Collier's *The Rise of Selfishness*, the blame for the terminal decline of our culture is assigned to the transition during the last century from a community-oriented citizenry to an overly self-oriented citizenry. This is a book by a confessed liberal who now thinks all of the wonderful "progressive" programs being pushed by government and the media did not really produce progress.[1] Significantly, he argues that the Victorian ethos—that is, the ideas, attitudes, and ideals that characterized Britain and the U.S. in the latter half of the nineteenth century—has been abandoned to our loss. He says, "The Victorians had roots; they had obligations; they had responsibilities. The essence of Victorianism was self-discipline and responsibility. Every man had a responsibility to his wife and children, to his forebears, to his community, to his nation, to his race, and he was expected to take all of these responsibilities seriously and to put them ahead of his personal self-interest. Having a strong sense of national and racial identity helped a man accept his responsibilities, but self-discipline was necessary too. Parents raised their children with this ethos in mind, not hesitating to apply external discipline, including corporal punishment, when needed. Thrift was a virtue, and waste a sin. People paid first for what they wanted to buy, not later. There were no credit cards. A man chronically in debt was a man whose honor was in jeopardy. Temperance and self-restraint also were virtues. A man constitutionally unable or unwilling to postpone self-gratification was held in low esteem."[2]

The most dangerous consequence Collier sees in the transition from Victorian virtues to a wholly self-centered population that has taken place in this last century is the utter destruction of the family. He looks at the trends—children growing up without fathers, working mothers putting consumerism ahead of proper parenting—and he warns, "We have seen an abandonment of parental responsibility which is unmatched in human history."[3] The disregard for law and contempt for authority have sprung from the trend to more selfishness. But the long-term impact is greatest on the essential building block of society—the family. "Increasingly younger people reject marriage, divorce easily, abandon their children, have fewer friends and see less of them…How do we explain this? In part it may have to do with the intense involvement with the media, which provide a substitute for human interaction…But at bottom, the increasing fragmentation of people is a consequence of the long-term turning inward to the self as the primary concern of life."[4] Another real consequence of the loss of thrift as a virtue is evidenced in the dilemma of old age. Can one support oneself? What is the role of personal savings, accumulated over a lifetime? Is there a value in not being a burden to others? In the current welfare state mentality most of this decision-making has been passed over to the state. In that sense the welfare state has removed actions from consequences.

Benjamin Franklin said: "If you would be wealthy, think of saving as well as getting." We could still benefit from that advice. Saving a part of what is earned—even a small part—is one way to build wealth. Consider two ways saving could help: Maintaining your own financial reserve for future expenses means you may not have to borrow money for those expenses or pay interest on that borrowed money. Reducing your borrowing occasions means fewer loan payments, so it is easier to maintain good credit. Americans have stopped saving for a rainy day. Instead, many people are living paycheck to paycheck, depending on credit cards to get them through emergencies, and hoping that the rising value of their homes will give them a retirement nest egg. Today's real estate morass and the resulting economic meltdown have seemingly taught us more about thrift in a few months than we had been willing to learn in the previous decade.

This personal economic chasm is showing up in the national savings rate, which has been declining for years. The U.S. Commerce Department reports that the personal savings rate fell to zero in 2008, the lowest since a one-month buying binge in the aftermath of the 9/11 attacks. The United States is on track to record a savings rate for

2009 below 1 percent, which would be the lowest since the depths of the Great Depression, when the rate turned negative. The nation's paucity of savings is raising alarms in many groups and institutions, from the Federal Reserve to consumer watchdogs, all worrying that the nation is counting on foreign savings to maintain a spendthrift lifestyle. Some groups are cranking up advertising campaigns to try to remind Americans that they don't need to participate in every sale.

And there are now high-level suggestions that the tax system needs to be changed to encourage savings instead of spending. "In two generations it seems that we've lost the culture and habit of savings," says the Consumer Federation of America. "There's so much marketing pressure to spend and buy and have instant gratification. And if you can't buy it now, put it on your credit card." Federal Reserve Chairman Alan Greenspan warned that the low savings rate is impairing the nation's long-term economic prospects. Economic common sense reminds us that an improved savings rate would provide investment money for businesses, which would create jobs.

Although Americans' savings are falling, their net worth is rising in large part because of soaring home prices and some improvement in the stock market (at least until recently, when both have fallen precipitously), so economists argue. People tend on average to spend about 6 percent of all housing market gains and 2 percent of their stock market gains, Naturally, when you have massive capital gains, you get people spending more, pushing the savings rate down. In fact, most analysts contend that the situation may not be as dire as the official statistics indicate. That is because when the Commerce Department calculates the savings rate, it doesn't include items such as capital gains and investments in pension plans.

Currently, there are about $12 trillion dollars in various structured retirement accounts not included in the savings rate. Assume that you bought a home and you held it for some number of years and you had a large capital gain. That capital gain would not be calculated as savings, and the taxes would be counted as an expense. So, even though you may look at the situation as though you have more savings than before, the Commerce Department does not. That said, a large proportion of Americans are not saving and have never saved.

This lack of saving is largely a function of income: Americans are just managing to survive as it is, and they don't have enough income to start saving. A recent Consumer Federation survey found the lack of savings was especially troublesome to women. More than 70 percent said they worried about their finances, and two thirds said that unexpected expenses—items such as the heater breaking or the car needing to be fixed—were the main cause of that worry. That is because they had little or no money set aside. More than 40 percent of all women had less than $500 in the bank. For those 25 to 34 years old, the percentage without a rainy day fund jumped to 55 percent. Since 1974 U.S. lawmakers have created about 20 separate tax breaks to encourage Americans to squirrel away more of their money. Yet over this time Americans have gone from saving about 10 percent of their disposable income to saving less than

1 percent. According to the latest data, Americans save as little as 40 cents for every $100 of disposable income.

For economic conservatives, these figures provide a heartening reminder that governments often fail to control human behavior. The trend is discouraging, and experts have been charged with finding new ways of encouraging Americans to save more. But some tax specialists believe that politicians are searching in vain for a policy that will lift the savings rate. So how big a problem is the low savings rate, and can policymakers do anything about it? On the surface, the decision of Americans not to save is perfectly rational. The appreciation of their houses and stock portfolios has been doing all the work for them, powering a $10 billion increase in net household wealth over the past few years, to $48,800 per household. Net wealth is now 550 percent of annual disposable income, comfortably above its average of 478 percent since 1952.

The worry for some economists, however, is that households may have placed far too much faith in capital gains. It seems that consumers have lost sight of the fact that past capital gains could easily turn into future capital losses. With house prices more overvalued at this time than in the housing booms of the 1970s and 1980s, we might expect outright falls, and indeed that is the case in certain overvalued locations worsened by the deepening recession.

Many economists are concerned that Americans could increase their savings and cut back spending with alarming speed if house prices stop rising, as they now have. The U.S. savings rate has been on a declining trend, but it is almost twice as volatile as the European savings rate. Few economists believe that the savings rate will bounce back to its long-term average of 7.4 percent. But even if Americans save at just half this rate they would need to set aside an additional $291 billion a year, which would lead to a full percentage point reduction in consumption growth for three years running.

All this testifies to an absence of thrift in America—a disposition to leave long-term provisions out of account. And this has led to another vulnerability: U.S. companies are being forced to look outside the country for the funds needed to invest. The ballooning current account deficit raises the risks of a sharp fall in the dollar and a rise in inflation and interest rates. Small wonder that lawmakers would like to see a gradual increase in savings. The chairman of Congress's joint economic committee seems undeterred by the apparent lack of success of previous savings incentives and has said. "We have tried hard to get people to save more but there are things we have not yet done." He thinks that the less we tax savings, the more people will save. He also argues that Americans will save more if they know that the cuts in dividend and capital gains tax introduced by President Bush are made permanent, since a lot of savings are still effectively taxed twice, once when they are earned and again when they yield a return.

Many experts, however, believe that adding still more generous incentives to save could paradoxically lower the national savings rate. The Urban Institute, a Washington think tank, thinks the extra tax breaks are unlikely to do more than lower government revenues. The institute's research has suggested that savings incentives merely encourage people to shift savings that would have been made any-way into tax-free vehicles. What we have at the moment, they argue, are incentives to deposit, not to save. Americans have certainly been putting a good deal of money into IRAs and 401Ks and getting tax breaks for doing so. But they have then been borrowing money on their homes or in other ways, canceling out the savings they have made.

Under this logic, further savings incentives will cost more in lost government revenues than they contribute to extra savings, thereby exacerbating the current account deficit. Many economists believe that only a radical shift to-ward a consumption tax, which would completely exclude any saved income from tax, would encourage more thrift. Such a move, however, would be vigorously opposed by most Democrats.

The evidence of the past 30 years is that the impact of tax incentives is dwarfed by larger economic forces, such as interest rates and the housing market. The incentive to save is largely determined by how wealthy you feel and the interest rate. Often it is not much consolation to be sav-ing on tax if you are barely earning any interest on your money. Ultimately the Federal Reserve, by putting up rates, is in a much better position to encourage saving than any other force.

Robert J. Samuelson, the leading economist in America, whose introductory textbook to economics many colleges still use, has said,

> "Every so often the government spits out some factoid that seems crammed with special signifi-cance. The Commerce Department did just that

recently when it reported that Americans' personal savings rate had dropped to zero. As a society, we seem unwilling to devote even a penny to the future. How could this be, considering all our huge contributions to retirement accounts? There are two possible answers. One is alarming: a low savings rate reflects national character—an addiction to immediate gratification. The other is more reassuring: low saving is partly a statistical mirage. Both answers are true."[5]

In recent years, the personal saving rate in the United States has fallen sharply, and it is now at a very low level compared either to U.S. historical experience or to the savings behavior of many other industrialized countries. Examining the causes and the consequences of the sharp decline in the U.S. personal saving rate, and whether there is reason to expect that it will remain low, is a critical research question. An understanding of these issues requires a look at how the personal saving rate is constructed and how it is affected by the household's perceived need to accumulate wealth to meet its future consumption needs.

The most frequently cited measure of the personal saving rate is based on the National Income and Product Accounts (NIPA). It is constructed by forming the ratio of Personal Saving to Disposable Personal Income (DPI), where DPI is defined as Personal Income (including wage and salary income, net proprietors' income, transfer payments less social insurance, income from interest and dividends, and net rental income) less tax and nontax payments to governments. Personal Saving is found by subtracting from DPI total Personal Outlays, most of which consist of Personal Consumption Expenditures (including consumer durables), with the remainder composed of Interest Paid by Persons (individuals, nonprofits, and trust funds) and Net Personal Transfer Payments to the Rest of the World. Given that personal saving is determined as a residual in the NIPA, measurement errors that appear anywhere in the computation of DPI or Personal Outlays will cumulate in personal savings.

In constructing the NIPA, the U.S. Commerce Department's Bureau of Economic Analysis (BEA) treats consistently the flow data associated with current production. As a result, the NIPA personal savings rate gives an incomplete picture of household savings behavior. For example, the NIPA measures of income and savings exclude the sale of or change in the market value of existing assets. For financial assets, personal income does include dividend and interest income to persons but excludes capital gains and losses. Therefore, the recent volatility in the stock market would not show up as changes in personal income and would not be included in the NIPA measure of personal savings. For nonfinancial assets of households, primarily housing and consumer durables, the NIPA includes service flows from housing as consumption but treats expenditures and not service flows from consumer durables as consumption. Similarly, personal expenditures on education and training are treated as consumption. These accounting practices overstate consumption and understate saving. Many recent studies of the decline in the personal savings rate focus on the other side of the coin, the consumption boom. That is, why has consumption as a percentage of disposable personal income been so high?

One explanation involves the "wealth effect," in which increases in the real value of assets stimulate consumption. The steep rise in the financial wealth of households beginning in the mid-1990s—which was principally due to the soaring stock market—is almost a mirror image of the falloff in the personal savings rate. Some argue that capital gains should be added to personal income, thus raising household savings and increasing the measured savings rate. Household wealth also includes tangible real assets, which constitute about one third of the household total asset holdings. The principal component of tangible assets is real estate, representing approximately 80% of the total. Like the stock market, housing prices also have appreciated, thus adding to household net worth and contributing to the decline in the personal saving rate. However, unlike the stock market, housing prices have not experienced sharp declines since the stock market peaked. During this period, the personal savings rate ceased its sharp decline but did not reverse course, until the steep market declines and fall in house values in late 2008. This suggests that while all of the dynamics of the wealth effect on consumption are playing themselves out, other factors also may have contributed to the low personal saving rate.

Another explanation for the sharp decline in the saving rate is associated with the coincident rise in labor productivity in the latter half of the 1990s. If households perceive that the higher labor income associated with this rise in productivity will continue into the future, then their permanent income, or the present value of future expected income, has increased, thus mitigating the need for additional saving out of current income. This argument would be consistent with the continued strength in aggregate productivity that has been in evidence in the data even during the current economic slowdown, when productivity improvements generally tend to fall off.

A third explanation is that financial innovation has relaxed liquidity constraints that many households had been facing by increasing their access to the credit markets. This argument is consistent with the observed increase in consumer credit relative to GDP that has accompanied the consumption boom. While this could be a significant contributing factor, the evidence put forward does not indicate that this is the principal factor propelling the consumption boom.

One concern that has been expressed over a low personal savings rate is that it may cause national savings to be insufficient to support the amount of investment necessary to sustain a high level of long-run economic growth without excessive dependence on foreign capital. Some concern also has been expressed that an unusually low personal savings rate may pose problems for the economy in the short run, if it were to be quickly reversed, thus representing fundamental behavioral instabilities in the economy. Such a view would be consistent with the notion that households have imprudently financed the consumption boom by running up an unsustainable level of consumer debt. Consider, for example, that the principal strength of the U.S. economy during the current recession (apart from housing) until recently has been the remarkable resilience of household consumption. Had there been a sudden unpredictable reversal of the personal savings rate, then, by definition, consumption would have fallen, which would have significantly exacerbated both the depth and duration of the current recession.

Substantial empirical evidence to date suggests that the low personal savings rate in the U.S. economy is a systematic response of households to changes in its fundamental determinants, most notably the increase in financial wealth. Had the stock market appreciation of the 1990s been the sole reason for the low personal savings rate, its decline would also portend weaker consumption. However, this effect would likely be spread out over several quarters, as some estimates of the wealth effect on consumption suggest. Moreover, it may also be the case that a lower personal savings rate will be a feature of the U.S. economy for the foreseeable future. This persistence could be attributed to an increase in trend productivity that induces higher permanent income for households or to a relaxation of financing constraints due to financial innovation. To the extent that these factors are important, the current low personal savings rate may not represent a large problem that is overhanging the U.S. economy but is instead a manifestation of a more efficient deployment of the economy's resources.

What we have seen, in other words, is the emergence over time of a new kind of capitalist economy. Instead of an economy based on saving and thrift, which launched Europe on its path of growth and prosperity and which we detailed earlier in this book, we have an economy based on consumption, debt, and credit, in which saving is discouraged not only by the culture of affluence but also by the fiscal policies of governments. It could be that this new economy, detached from the virtues of thrift, temperance, and prudence, will maintain itself indefinitely. It could be that the real consequences will be seen not in the form of economic instability or recession but in the gradual corrosion of civil society as long-term planning and commitment give way to short-term gratification. It could be that we are witnessing the proof that, while thrift may not after all be necessary to a capitalist economy, it is fundamental to the moral life, and that these two entities—prosperity and moral order—which have hitherto supported each other, are now finally coming apart.

## CHAPTER FIVE

# The "Spirit" of Nations

*"Industry, thrift and self-control are not sought because they create wealth, but because they create character."*
—Calvin Coolidge

The corruption of the thrift economy and its replacement by the economy of consumption have many causes, not all of them reversible. But one cause should certainly be considered, since it lies within the power of all of us to do something about it, and that is the rise of the centralized state and its steady expropriation of social life. The administrative state has in modern times crowded out the individual and the mediating structures to such an extent that there is no longer what Abraham Kuyper, a nineteenth-century Dutch prime minister, called "sphere sovereignty"—that is to say, the sovereignty of the institutions, associations, and endeavors of civil society, each of which is able to take charge of its own proper sphere. While families, friendly societies, churches, and local associations used to look after the poor, the lonely, the sick, and the distressed, the state now takes charge, providing material support but enhancing the loneliness. How did we come to the point that we look to the State for all our welfare, protection, and regulation? And why is it justified? What would Jefferson and his allies say about creeping state power and the idea of (un)limited government? Can the State be limited again? States are notoriously bad at thrift because they appropriate for political ends, rarely rescind bad decisions, and have no conception of public savings. The only activities they appear to do well are spend, tax, and grow.

The State has certainly become supreme, for it alone is now viewed as sovereign. People look to the State for solutions to problems in every sphere of life. The State has taken over the definition of virtue and in the process destroyed much of our sense of individual responsibility. Such a State is rarely thrifty, because it is constantly looking for more control and more programs to administer. A full-orbed discussion about national security in the broadest sense can therefore be both enlightening and disturbing, for it clarifies the magnitude of the challenges to any community based on transcendence in an era where we have, to use the political philosopher Eric Voegelin's phrase, "immanentized the eschaton" and localized our ideals in territorial national entities. It amplifies and reinforces the struggle identified by St. Augustine as that between the City of God and the City of Man.

Erastianism is a doctrine named after a sixteenth-century Swiss theologian, Thomas Erastus, who argued for the State's control of spiritual and ecclesiastical matters. The idea was dramatically implemented by Henry VIII, who declared that he, not the pope, was supreme head of the Church in England. The supremacy of secular power was influentially defended by Richard Hooker in his treatise of

1594, *Ecclesiastical Polity*. The political theory and practice of the Western world tell the story of a growing Erastianism, in which the modern state, brooking no competition from other claims to sovereignty, has attempted to eliminate the "boundary disputes" between temporal and spiritual authorities. The United States in its founding, as is evident in the Religion Clause of the First Amendment, is the great exception to this general pattern. But "American exceptionalism," also on this score, needs constantly to be reexamined and, when necessary, defended. Without limits, the State drives out prophetic religion and establishes a monopoly on public space and public meanings. That is the circumstance referred to as "the naked public square." As Father Richard Neuhaus always reminded us, we must never tire of recalling, because it does not remain naked but is taken over by the pseudo-religion established by state power.

However, any critique of the present state of affairs should not attack the State *per se*. We need to acknowledge that God and nature have established the State's role to function explicitly as an arm of common grace, both with regard to its authority to wield the sword and its authority to make and administer laws in the pursuit of justice. And we should be careful to point out the Biblical truth that the power extended to the State is always to be guided and ruled by *law*. The two elements, power and law, are to be balanced like a seesaw, with law as a constant constraint and regulator. Recognizing that inherent pride is the greatest force undermining the ability of humans to resolve their (international) differences peacefully, we could also acknowledge from the outset that possibly the biggest need in the development of worldwide security may be a large dose of "cosmic humility." But that is often hard to come by or has proven difficult to manufacture because of national selfishness.

The centralization and corruption of the State have not come about by accident. They are the result of a complex historical process, whereby people's loyalties have been reshaped in secular rather than religious terms. The State has grown as an idol as faith in God has weakened. And the welfare state displays the nadir of this process, the point where spiritual capital has been entirely absorbed into the State, to be squandered by people who are in no way answerable to the future generations that depend on our thrift. Such, I believe, is what we see all around us in the developed world.

But to understand this situation we must inquire further into the very rise of the nation state and its role in offering a vision of satisfaction and security. The present situation and norms surrounding nations make little or no sense to many people, in the developed countries or the developing world: North or South, East or West, Islamic, Christian, Hindu, Jewish, Buddhist, or secular.

Making sense of so-called international relations and the security of nations requires two essential tools: (1) learning to cope with an enormous amount of contradictory information, some of which is extremely difficult, if not impossible, to verify and confirm; and (2) learning to contextualize this information, because it is not objective. It always needs interpretation. As the theologian Martin Buber said, "The greater the crisis becomes the more earnest and consciously responsible is the knowledge demanded for us. For although what is demanded is a deed, only the deed born of the knowledge of Christ will overcome the crisis." [1]

What constitutes a nation, anyway, in the new century before us? What makes any of the nearly 200 nation states a *State* in the first place? Few questions have been more contested in modern times. The answers depend on the views of the answerers: Rousseau differs from Fichte, Mazzini from Wilson, Ben-Gurion from Nasser, Nehru, Mao, or Castro. Some have argued that common language is the root of the nation; others, common history or common ideals. Hans Kohn in his seminal work, *Nationalism*, writes, "Nationalism is a state of mind, in which the supreme loyalty of the individual is felt to be due the nation-state." [2] A deep attachment to one's native soil, to local traditions, and to established territorial authority has existed in varying strength throughout much of human history. But it was not until the end of the eighteenth century that nationalism and national security, in the modern sense of those terms, became a generally recognized sentiment, increasingly molding *all* of public and private life.

Nationalism and its corollary, national security, when reified (so that the abstract concept is treated as if it is a concrete reality), can quickly become an *ism*; it becomes an ideology and all that that implies. All nationalism is inseparably linked to modernity; ours has become the age of nationalisms. Only in Europe over the past two centuries, and predominantly now in the twentieth and twenty-first centuries, have people identified themselves *totally* with the nation, civilization with national civilization, and their life and survival with the life and survival of their particular nationality. From the late eighteenth century, nationalism has in fact dominated the impulses and attitudes of the masses and, at the same time, served as the justification for the State to use its force against its own citizens and against other nation states. Only in England and in France, especially during the Revolution of 1789, did the state cease to be the king's estate and become the people's state, a national state, a fatherland. From that point, the people were responsible for their country's destiny. Nation *and* state were one, hence the very nomenclature "nation state."

Against the common, general, universal unity arose this new nationalism that glorified the peculiar and the parochial. National differences and national individualities became more important than anything else. Spiritually, nationalism is quintessentially modern in the sense that God was removed from the scene, and with His disappearance, any divine plan for all things was forgotten. Moreover, the will of the people (i.e., Rousseau's "general will") became authoritative for forming political and economic units and for ruling. This continues to be the basic idea of the nation. In effect, the glory of the nation has by now nearly fully replaced the glory of God (or of the King) as a unifying value or agent. The nation state, be it the collective state, Nazi Reich, Mazzini's united Italy, Zionist Israel, the Communist People's China, or the federal state (as in the United States), has become the principal political reality of the modern age. Nations, pretended, imagined, and real, are the mortal gods of secular culture.

What actually is the modern nation state? What beliefs make up nationalism, from which the concept of national security is derived? The literature is replete with different elements and concepts of nationhood. Let us list a number of them here that deserve special consideration:

- a certain defined area or territory, either possessed or coveted;

- a common culture, language, customs, manners, and literature;

- a set of common, dominant social and economic institutions and practices;

- an independent, sovereign government, the principle that each nation is completely separate from every other;

- a belief in a common history, even myths, and common origin, sometimes racial in nature;

- a love or esteem for fellow nationals, not necessarily as individuals but as a group;

- a common pride in achievements (military more than others) and sorrow in tragedies

- a disregard for or hostility toward other groups, especially if they seem to threaten or prevent the separate national existence; and

- a hope that the nation will have a great and glorious future in territorial expansion or in supremacy (i.e., as a world power—militarily, culturally, or financially).

Nationalism is indeed a very complex and rich concept; it certainly defies being captured by a short, logical definition. In essence, nationalism signifies a sentiment that unifies people and is expressed in real devotion and loyalty to *that* nation state, and its absolute security, whatever the government in power. In its most ardent form, it requires, as Rousseau advocated, absolute devotion to and conformity with the *will* of the nation as expressed by the rulers. Nationalism demands the supremacy of the nation to which one belongs to such a degree that security becomes a primary or even the exclusive focus of national behavior.

Over time, numerous illusions have grown up around the nation state and national security. Some people have believed that their nation is a creation of God, that they alone have supernatural powers. Others have seen nations as determined by soil or rooted in race, blood, and tribal existence. Still others have argued that their nation is the product of a demand for markets or status or the end result of class warfare or the struggle for power. All of these ideas and their historical manifestations are gross oversimplifications at best, the product of fanatics at worst. In fact, our present understanding does not reveal any of these differences as the basis for exclusion. To do so is to proceed at the expense of truth and at mankind's great peril, as World Wars I and II amply demonstrate.

Hans Kohn, the foremost authority on the topic, has said, "In this time of mental and verbal confusion when general political terms have become so emotionally fraught that they cover disparate realities, we have to start re-thinking many concepts in the interest of human freedom and the possibility of cultural intercourse."[3] And Eric Fromm in *Sane Society* excoriates national interest and security as "our incest, our idolatry, our insanity."[4]

We must say that if men are not compatible, it is not because they inherently differ in nature or in biology. That sentiment of unity and exclusiveness we have defined as nationalism, and its concrete and more subtle form—national security—does not mean that persons could not in principle live in the world more peaceably. For there is no historical, biological, or psychological basis for believing that nationalism or the security of any given nation must or will be permanent. Far below the surface of national peculiarities, however, humans are far more alike than we are different. For we all bear the image of God, and the fall did not eradicate our common bonds. This is the transcendent truth. And some of our differences—cultural, linguistic, and otherwise post-Babel—may actually be good; that is not being questioned. We are nevertheless God's image bearers, and only in that relationship do we find eternal security. A polyglot world contains linguistic pleasures unavailable in a monoglot world, but it is a bit of a stretch to say that Babel simply instituted "diversity." Didn't it rather institute confusion? The men of Babel were punished for their egoism. Sure, out of the punishment of confusion comes the joy of diversity. God's law leads to God's grace. This is worth clarifying. Pentecost is often seen as the undoing of the Babel curse, but if all that Babel brought about was diversity, why was it considered a curse?

What then are the causes of war? Whether a political culture is liberal, conservative, fascist, or communist, today it thinks of itself in *national* terms. Nationalism and national security have become the most important elements in modern politics. And the most pressing matter in the entire field of national security is the cause of war. War today takes many forms, between many actors, not all of them nation states. Terrorism has reshaped our very definitions of risk, security, and war or conflict itself.

Why is political controversy so often violent? The pages of history, from one angle, appear to be almost totally covered with blood. War has been called an international disease, a collective insanity, a gross malfunction, and a global conspiracy. Others, however, find it completely rational and just, even inevitable. According to Carl von Clausewitz, the Prussian paragon of military strategy, "War is not merely a political act, but also a real political instrument, a continuation of political commerce, a carrying out of the same by other means."[5]

War, that organized conduct of major armed hostilities between social groups and nations (including civil war and international conflict), has many causes, from so-called power asymmetries to arms races that get out of control; from nationalism, separatism, and irredentism (the "need" to recover lost ancestral territory) to instinctual aggression; from the need to create a common enemy to relative deprivation. However one chooses to explain the causes of war, the many theories agree on one point: There has never been a deadlier game invented by human beings.

Between 1939 and 1945 more than 60 million people (over 3 percent of the world's population) died as a result of World War II. It was the greatest single catastrophe in human history. And the most destructive nuclear weapons were used only in the closing days of that war. Today, nuclear weapons have become the major factor in the arsenals of an increasing number of super-powerful nations. But even the existence of thousands of these nuclear weapons has not prevented nonnuclear wars. At least 15 significant wars have been fought since 1945, and the United States participated in four of them.

Nation states spend a great deal of their time preparing or planning to fight wars. These wars are costly and divert spending from other good uses. The total expenditures of all countries on weapons now exceed a trillion dollars per year and continue to rise rapidly. By one estimate, 280 wars have been fought between 1648 and 2005, or one every 1.4 years,[6] and acts of terrorism running into the many thousands are not even counted in these tabulations. Clearly, war remains the most outstanding problem of the twenty-first century. Although there is no explicit reference to what share of GNP should be dedicated to defense or security, historically this percentage has grown or shrunk in proportion to perceived threats and the power of various interests, including those of a geographical nature, where bases were located or production facilities founded. Normatively, the question of the proper share of resources devoted to national defense and security needs to be comparatively examined in the light of other domestic considerations and global needs. Surely there exists a strong and growing need for security and just defense in a world of turmoil, uncertainty, and unprecedented risk, but just how much is open to debate.

Contrast the realities of modern war and the less-than-thrifty expenditures for it with what we find in the prophet Micah 4:2-3 (NIV): "The law will go out from Zion, the word of the Lord from Jerusalem. He will judge between many peoples and will settle disputes for strong nations far and wide. They will beat their swords into plowshares and their spears into pruning hooks. Nation will not take up sword against nation, nor will they train for war anymore." The list of prophetic testimonies, like the Psalter and the entire Exodic tradition, sees politics and security exclusively in terms of justice and peacekeeping. In Scripture, justice and peacemaking were often first undertaken for the poor and the oppressed. It is reassuring today to remember that judgment belongs to God-He, Yahweh (the eschatological significant name in Hebrew that says, "I will be"), who liberates His people. All justice and peacemaking are therefore a concrete embodiment of the will of God.

The State is the central actor in international relations. But how can we normatively approach these inter-state relations in an area as complicated as national security and relations between all-powerful states? A number of answers are presented and discussed in Martin Rein's *Social Science and Public Policy.*[7] For example, he suggests that we can treat policy questions as unresolved, as too ambiguous and conflicting, in what he calls the empiricist approach. We can examine policy only in its historical perspective, as do the historicists. We can distrust any orthodoxy, as the skeptics are likely to do. We can consider the political reception of various policy options as pragmatists, asking only what will work. Or we can approach national security as moral critics, highlighting the difference between what men believe and what they actually do. This sort of witness may be most appealing to those who believe in normativeness. But norms of knowledge are not used simply to influence policy. The process is more complex; as policy evolves, norms are also used to selectively justify actions. So policy and norms are interactive, being as much influenced by the current agenda. This is what could be called a norm-critical approach. Joan Robinson, the economic theorist, captured the essence of this approach when she said, "It is impossible to describe a system without moral and religious judgments creeping in. For to look at a system from the outside implies that it is not the only possible system. In describing it we compare it, openly or tacitly, with other actual or imagined systems. Differences imply choices, and choices imply judgments. We cannot escape from making judgments and the judgments we make arise from the ethical and religious preconceptions that have soaked into our view of life."[8]

My point is that it is not only sterile to pursue the techniques of analysis divorced from issues of purpose but also misleading, because techniques arise to serve purposes and these rest on normative assumptions. Beliefs attach themselves to means as much as they do to ends; beliefs about what is normative or just are tied up with acceptable, feasible, operating procedures. So for our purposes, and using the jargon of the policy sciences, policies (including national security policies) are interdependent systems of cherished abstract norms; operating principles that give these norms form in the context of specific programs and institutional arrangements; outcomes of programs enabling us to contrast ideals with reality; linkages (weak and strong ones) between aims, means, and outcomes; and feasible strategies and tactics of change.

In other words, policies always reaffirm an ethical, moral, or spiritual position. As decision-makers, critics, citizens, or policy analysts, we must look at the respective policies and recover the consciousness of created reality and use it as the foundation for all public policy. This call is imperative in our era of Gnostic futurisms, in which the *Alpha* of the creation has been repudiated to make possible the realization of a secular *Omega*, a massive shift in eschatology. We must see national security issues from the perspective of creation and analyze all public policies from this normative point of view. If we do not, others will use their perverted world views as the point of policy departure and shape the policies for us.

Several different dimensions that need to be seen together if a complete picture is to be rendered characterize the present global system. Externally, the state system involves international relations, the rules it employs (i.e., diplomacy), and the games (including war) it uses to meet its ends. Internally, the nation state is a reflection of a given state's domestic nature. Some states are capitalistic; some are socialistic. Some nations are developed; some are less developed, economically. Some states are democratic; some are authoritarian or totalitarian. In today's world, some states are religiously fanatic; others have disestablished state religions or are blatantly secular in their outlook. Some states sponsor terrorist actions. Finally, national security is itself always part of a given decision-making process. Policy often depends as much on those who administer it as it does on procedures. History records this fact for all who care to look at the details.

Only by analyzing each level can we have a comprehensive view of the "games nations play." Why they play, how they play, and how they regulate, moderate, or even try to abolish the game they play differ from nation to nation. This is especially true in a policy area as critical as national security, where each facet is a layer unto itself and where the stakes are so high, often revolving around survival itself.

The current world situation actually presents three alternative scenarios: (1) a world in constant national conflict; (2) a world of international legal conformity; or (3) a world of pluralistic and diverse social systems striving to avoid fatal collisions. We must choose and work for the third option while we strive to allow all peoples to participate in human dignity in choosing, by democratic means, their own leaders and integrating themselves into the global, now largely capitalistic, economy. By showing respect for the diversity instituted at Babel we honor creation by exercising our task to live in a world community while we avoid the dangers and sin of nationalism and maintain the rich diversity of our various cultures. The distinction between a patriot who loves his particular national culture and one with excessive patriotism should be borne in mind. Barbara Ward in her classic book, *Five Ideas that Changed the World,* argues that the stronger the nationalism, theirs or ours, the greater the risk for all of us.[9] Is it time to consider the consequences not of nations or the spirit of nations but our excessive nationalism? Unfortunately, as Harry Blaimers suggests in his telltale book, *The Christian Mind*, "Except over a very narrow field of thinking, chiefly touching on questions of personal conduct, Christians in the modern world accept, for the purpose of mental activity, a frame of reference constructed by the secular mind. There is no Christian mind; there is no shared field of discourse in which we can move at ease as thinking Christians by trodden ways and past established landmarks." [10] This fact is frightfully clear when it comes to discussions about nations and security.

Embarking on this difficult path, where our subject is a policy of national security, demands that we realize, at the outset, that our subject involves the international relations among states. That means we must have a proper understanding of the State itself. The State is characterized by its unique empowerments—that is, it has a monopoly on governing in a given territory. The State also has the sanction to exercise power and to make laws. Power alone does not explain these prerogatives. Because the State is sanctioned (by God), "realpolitik" does not exhaust a normative understanding of power relations. Rather, the State's juridical function must guide the functions of power in a proper understanding of international relations and national security. Might and right are intrinsic. Might must be guided by right. Law is the qualifying idea of the State. And law exists to order, define, and ensure justice.

I would define the State as a public, legally organized community of government and subjects with a dual purpose that embodies legal jurisdiction and legal protection, the ends of which are public justice. International relations are concerned about the relations among such states. And if states exist to bring about justice, it follows that the dominant concern of international relations ought to be the true norm of international justice. This concept has serious consequences for formulation of security policy and policies on every subject of interest to a foreign ministry or a national security council, from legitimate defense to foreign assistance, from intervention or economic relations to the conduct of diplomacy.

People of virtue or faith in various traditions have something to say to the world of international relations and national security policy because they have a special view of the world: who made it, what sustains and preserves it, and what true justice is. Different from liberalism, and the view of individual self-interests; different from realism, and notions of the balance of power, different from Marxism, and deterministic theories of class struggle; and different from fascism, which glorifies national expansion and aggression, faith possesses a unique idea of justice to be concretized in, not abstracted from, reality.

Following this argument, we need to focus on what could be called the principles or norms for national security policy. As already noted, we live in a world of nation states and must, at all costs, avoid zealous nationalism. This distinction is imperative for people of faith, who have allegiances beyond and transcending those of a territorial definition. By normative, I mean the quality of an action estimated by a standard of right and wrong, true and untrue, just and unjust. There are, after all, only three choices in this regard. Persons and states can purposely choose to be moral (even based on a set of religious norms), amoral, or immoral. God's admonition is to love our neighbors as ourselves. What might that mean for national security policy?

The debate between Realpolitik and Normativeness is decades old and has had proponents on both sides. Many key persons involved in guiding foreign policy and national security policy today argue that national interests (self-interests) alone can be the valid rationale for policy. This position, known as the "realist school" of international relations, holds that relations among states are amoral. Realists, reacting against the utopianism and idealism of earlier times, do not believe much cooperation is possible among nation states, and they certainly do not believe morality can bring it about. Instead they assert that conflict is the hallmark of politics, particularly world politics, and that all nation states seek to advance their own interests, exclusive of others, and do so through the exercise of sheer power.

I cannot accept the realists' strict dichotomy between morality or normativeness and national interest. Such thinking is not only erroneous but also dangerous and unbiblical. We can consider two alternative normative propositions for national security and public policy. First, normative questions cannot be separated from questions of national security and are, in fact, an integral part of the foreign policy-making process, which implies that every policy is based on a set of principles disclosed or undisclosed. Second, policies need to be shaped and judged by ultimate principles or norms—including biblical ones such as justice, freedom, mercy, and peace. They should not be shaped in some forced majoritarian sense or through coer-

cion. They ought to be formulated in the context of a pluralistic political culture and in a spirit of tolerance.

We should then include in our discussion of nationalism a critique of the realist school, which is so dominant. Its
primary theorists are George Kennan, Hans Morgenthau,
Henry Kissinger, and Reinhold Niebuhr, a so-called
Christian realist. Realists argue that the center or essence of
international and national security is the concept of *interest,* defined in terms of power. A successful foreign policy
enhances national power and national security at any cost.
And the international system (and its regional parts, including the global economy) turns into a system of conflict instead of political cooperation. To quote Kennan, "morality
must be rejected. Other criteria, sadder, more limited, more
practical must be allowed to prevail."[11]

This question needs to be answered: Are national interests or are normative principles (universal standards,
biblical standards, and natural laws, spiritual wisdom) to be
the bases for shaping national security and foreign policy
for the world's nation states? A real confusion fostered by
the apologists of realpolitik is their plea for the recognition
of war as a necessary arm of national security policy. By accepting war and strategies based primarily on conflict, and
thereby their unquestioned legitimacy, realists in the nuclear era are involved in a near absurdity. Moreover, the intellectual effort to preserve the struggle for power as the bed-
rock of political reality makes little sense in conditions of
"total war." Zbigniew Brzezinski elaborated on this point in
his book *In Quest of National Security Policy,* where he quoted

from a speech on the strategic implications of "Thou shalt not kill," while reflecting on the concept of national security. He said, "Moral choices are involved in the interplay of states, and historical outcomes are infused with moral consequences. Outcomes in the interplay of power are not morally neutral. Moral choices should also affect the means used in international competition, including even the exercise of force."[12]

At the outset, the realists may be correct in pointing to the tendency of each state to identify its own interest with universal principles through a rationalization process that is often self-deceptive. But this warning can be accepted while still rejecting exclusive national interest as the only, final guide for policy. Most certainly we must do this or risk becoming idolatrous. The idea of national interest embodies two major problems. First, empirically there is rarely such a thing as the single national interest; usually there are many interests and often competing ones. Second, governments are composed of individual persons, each with his or her own personality, interests, and priorities. National interest can be thought of broadly to identify with the interests of the community or narrowly to promote self-serving goals, even to serving individual leaders in a "cult of personality." National interest in this sense can be most problematic and unthrifty; relational compassion and justice are better alternatives.

In the final analysis, national or state interest has been used, even manipulated, to mean all kinds of things to all sorts of people. But from my perspective, the preservation of any one state cannot be raised to the level of an absolute imperative. And in modernity, no nation state is the equivalent of ancient Old Testament Israel, a chosen people. Some states historically have been more or less just than other states. So, too, have some states been more belligerent than others. Arguably, only God is sovereign. Therefore, the pursuit of a single national interest as the highest responsibility of statesmen or citizens should be rejected. None other than the apologist C. S. Lewis said, "Finally we reach the stage where patriotism in its demoniac form unconsciously denies itself. We all know now that this love becomes a demon when it becomes a god."[13] This does not mean that nationals of any given country should not love their home, their birthplace, their language, or their way of life. Far from it, for as Gilbert Chesterton declares, "A man's reasons for not wanting his country to be ruled by foreigners are very much like his reasons for not wanting his house to be burned down, because he could not even begin to enumerate all the things he would miss."[14]

Where does all of this leave us? Completely lost? Not if we think about and act on what we deeply believe. All areas of life, not only individual behavior but also world politics, are filled with both evil and opportunity for good. Likewise, every area confronts us with a host of normative choices. Personal life and national life are full of difficult questions about the use of force, charity, discipline, intervention, allocation of resources, and so on. The fact that hard choices have to be made is no reason to ignore normative answers. Somebody's ideology, values, or religion is going to provide these answers in the final analysis.

How then, do we take what appear to be rather abstract, even spiritual norms and apply them to concrete situations in policy areas as forbidding as national security? Or how do we establish priorities for competing principles or strategies, even the virtue of thrift? These tentative suggestions seem appropriate. Norms can and should serve as a guide in political decision-making as well as in private matters, even if followed imperfectly and unevenly. After all, every policy and goal of political action, from international security policy to domestic welfare policy, are ultimately determined by a set of values. The question is: Which values or virtues take precedence? We should try to enunciate values and see to it that political "actors" have the chance to hear these standards and consider them so they can be made part of the debate. But we must at the same time be wary of the tendency of all persons and nations (including ourselves) to elevate their own ideals, institutions, and practices to the level of immutable laws of the universe or count themselves alone as God's chosen people. There is no room for self-infused nationalism, self-righteousness, or an aggressive spirit. These are all indefensible. Realizing that nation states are established and called to "bring forth" justice, we can work to have national structures that promote them and organize people in ways encouraging them to follow such norms. In this sense, nation states that do not practice nationalism in one of the historical excessive forms are pregnant with possibilities for the establishment of justice.

Psalm 100 could be read focusing on the world of nation states and national security in the coming decades:

"Make a joyful noise unto the Lord, all ye lands. Serve the Lord with gladness: come before his presence with singing. Know ye that the Lord he is God: it is he that hath made us, and not we ourselves; we are his people, and the sheep of his pasture. Enter into his gates with thanksgiving, and into his courts with praise: be thankful unto him, and bless his name. For the Lord is good; his mercy is everlasting; and his truth endureth to all generations."

The spiritual ideals expressed in Psalm 100 may have been good for King David and people in the primitive Middle Eastern cultures, or possibly even in the so-called Dark Ages, but are such hopes and aspirations possible today? A.J.P. Taylor, the noted English historian, wrote, "Religious strength has lost its strength. Not only has church-going declined, but also the dogma of revealed religion—the Incarnation and Resurrection—is believed by only a small number. Christ has become, even for many avowed Christians, merely the supreme example of a good man. This is a great happening in history...few remain Christians in morality, even fewer keep the faith."[15]

I have here argued that normatively grounded moral choices rooted in spirituality, what I call a *spirit of nations*, must be woven into the very fabric of foreign and national policy-making. Choices must be evaluated in terms of norms that we understand to be those emerging from a normative basis, informed by reason. We need to start connecting these norms with national security policy and thinking. There is no guarantee that this task will be easy or meet with quick success. Furthermore, equally committed persons may disagree with one another.

Humility and tolerance will have to be exercised, but the scriptures in all faith traditions also call us to be peacemakers and to attend to the needs of the poor. The vision of the good allows us to work for justice, freedom, and peace; to bring help to the poor; and to free the captives. We are required as individuals and in community to do no less in our lives as members of nation states. Only in doing so can we transform what has become the often-misdirected *spirit of nations* into the spirituality of all people. Only then can we rejoin the argument about thrift and the other virtues in our public lives.

I am not alone in making this argument. Christopher Dawson offered it decades ago and Michael Burleigh has made it more recently in his cogent twin works, *Earthly Powers* and *Sacred Causes*. Like both of them, I see the central tragedy of modernity in the "Moloch-like" expansion of the modern state. It has nearly colonized all areas of life, including morality. In fighting back we must reclaim both our individual freedom and the preservation of a sphere beyond the state that anticipates civil society, exhibits elected leadership, and holds rulers accountable to higher standards. The place is the Church, and in this civilization, particularly in our darkest hours, it has sustained the West and its notion of virtue.

## CHAPTER SIX

# Modern Theories and Institutions of Thrift

*"Be thrifty, but not covetous."*
—Benjamin Franklin

In modern-day management theory and financial and investment strategy there is very little mention of thrift. Are you surprised? The term is either used pejoratively or simply excused altogether. There are a few exceptions. Thomas Stewart, the management guru, recently suggested in "12 Management Tips for Slow Times," that thrift, "that quaint Calvinist virtue could be the 'first-mover' advantage of the 21st century."[1] He actually advocates thrift. Since profits are down and demand sags, Stewart says, "Companies should turn to austerity."[2] He says, "The future no longer belongs to the irrationally exuberant, but to companies that demonstrate, quarter in and quarter out, the ability to produce and sell more without burning through people, capital, and other resources. The grand strategic challenge, the one real leaders set for themselves, is to use lean times like this to transform a company into an organization that knows in its bones how to do more with less—not just now, but forever."[3]

We do hear almost every day about negative savings rates, record current account deficits, big budget deficits, a falling U.S. dollar, rising prices of oil and other commodities due to our insatiable demand, and huge outflows of our currency to the reserve accounts of the likes of China and Japan. None of this is typically rerouted back to thrift or austerity. What is also forgotten is America's productivity. From 2000 to 2006 the workforce of the largest 500 American companies rose by a mere 3.6 percent while revenue increased by nearly 40 percent. Profits rose by a whopping 80 percent, all of which demonstrates that more output, revenue, and sales were gained essentially from the same resources. This productivity gain is thrift's secret; it brings discipline, drives the bottom line, and provides investors and managers alike with the result of thrifty decisions made over a long period of time. Here corporate frugality and prudent investment are a means to an end and the vision or a story of what it is, where it is going, and why it's worth the pain to get there.

It was not always so. It was the wish of one Reverend Henry Duncan in rural Scotland to do something of real and lasting value for the underprivileged that led to the beginning of the first savings bank, which over time grew into a worldwide movement. He believed deeply in the dignity of the ordinary working man. Wherever he saw injustice he worked and spoke against it. Despite the appalling poverty of the time, he was totally against the introduction of a poor rate (poverty level), something he fought against all his life, believing subsidies were degrading and did nothing to create a spirit of pride and independence.

Despite his successful efforts at revival, he was not satisfied that the Friendly Society was the final answer to the problem of poverty. Drawing on the experience gained during the three years he had spent working in Heywood's Bank in Liverpool, and with his knowledge of savings schemes already tried but found wanting, he concluded that a savings bank could succeed only if it was self-supporting and based on business principles. He succeeded in gaining the backing of the heritors or landowners, who must have welcomed the idea that the poor might no longer need their support. Realizing the value of publicity, six months before he opened his bank he founded a local newspaper, *The Dumfries & Galloway Courier*, in which he published his proposal for a parish bank in Ruthwell.

In 1810 in the Society Room in Ruthwell Duncan put to his parishioners his ideas for a parish bank. The established banks needed £10 to open an account; in Ruthwell sixpence was enough. The deposits were placed with the Linen Bank in Dumfries and received 5 percent interest. Members received 4 percent interest, on whole pounds. The surplus provided a charity fund, tiered interest for long-term savers, and a sum for administering the bank. All the administration in Ruthwell was done by the Minister himself. Instead of taking any remuneration, Henry Duncan used the money due to him to build another school in the parish. Maintaining Henry Duncan's vision, each year Lloyds TSB still provides the Lloyds TSB charity foundations with 1 percent of that banking group's pretax profits averaged over three years.

Within five years of the bank opening in Ruthwell, there were savings banks throughout the U.K.; the following year they spread to Europe and the United States. During that first year the total savings amounted to £151. Ten years later in the United Kingdom the total had reached over three million pounds. A theology of thrift led to the institutionalization of savings for all people, not just the wealthiest.

A parish minister in a small Scottish town encouraged thrift in his congregation and began to collect more than tithes.[4] Similar institutions sprang up in Australia, New Zealand, and America, mostly out of a religious impetus. By the 1850s these thrift banks became involved in an activity that has become one of the most sought after, mortgage finance. Later trends included self-reliance and planning toward saving for retirement, education, and, of course, more sophisticated investment advice. Most of the advancements made in savings over the last two centuries would probably be beyond the comprehension of the early founders of thrift institutions. But the reasons for savings, rooted in the concept of thrift, remain the same—to serve communities, to help people and families to grow and to preserve their wealth. Twenty-first century wealth management and complex, diversified portfolios are a long way from rural church-based savings, but the rationale remains virtually the same.

This brings us to the so-called *paradox of thrift*. There is a raging debate in many countries around the world about whether people are saving enough for their own good. The importance of saving is rarely debated. But since it involves the sacrifice of consumption today for the sake of future benefits, it is difficult for a household, a business, or a government to decide on the proper or appropriate rate of saving. Saving behavior has important national and macroeconomic implications that ultimately affect all citizens beyond the realm of their own domestic financial management. It influences the overall performance of an economy and therefore national prosperity and economic growth. Adam Smith himself, in his *Wealth of Nations*, argued the virtue of saving as the key to economic progress.[5] Contrast this with John Maynard Keynes, who in his *General Theory of Employment, Interest, and Money* saw a high savings rate as far from a virtue, actually undermining prosperity.[6] His argument became the basis of the celebrated *Paradox of Thrift*. Arguing for more government spending, Keynes was an opponent to thrift. He once said, "The expectation of profits, not abstinence, was the engine that drives enterprise." For him thrift was a miserly virtue, if a virtue at all. It was fine for conditions of scarcity but had no place in an age of prosperity. Actually John Hobson had made this point long before, challenging the orthodoxy that savings and investment went together. If people saved too much, he thought it would lead to underconsumption, even declining investment. Economists have debated for decades about some magic number or formula for the level of savings in a given country. While there are many sides and positions, most see today's savings rates as too low. Further, there is general agreement that there are often obstacles in an economy in the way the financial and tax systems bias individuals and companies toward consumption and away from saving. Removing these inefficiencies and obstacles, it is argued, is of paramount importance, so that people and companies can make clear, rational, and informed choices about the appropriate level of savings.

Wealth creation and civil society are joined at the hip. Without a prospering and robust economy based in freedom it is difficult, if not impossible, to bring civil society into being. The antecedent to the emergence of civil society is a society of the heroic-imperial type. There have been quite a number of these, enough to justify the hypothesis that it is somehow the default option of humankind. Think of the great and small empires of biblical times: Assur, Egypt, Babylon, Persia, and Rome. There we encounter warring tribes and cities, and every now and then one tribe or city becomes the dominant power and develops into something called an *empire*. This political situation is reflected in ancient interpretations of the universe itself and especially of the gods: The universe is often portrayed as the result of a primordial war between different gods, and the gods continue to be experienced as warriors.

Historically, we encounter several attempts to break away from this heroic-imperial constellation. The first is definitely Israel's exodus—an event very much underrated in the history of political ideas. Another, much later attempt in the classical world, both Greek and Roman, is what Aristotle coined as *koinonia politike* and Cicero later called *societas civilis*, phrases that are the ancestors of our present-day term "civil society." Characteristic of these attempts is the conviction that the well-being of the political community is the responsibility of each citizen. However, the notion of well-being, and therefore well-doing, is deeply colored by a moral horizon in which the honor and glory of the city remains pivotal. This implies that the institutional energy is focused on society as a whole, which should be powerful and honorable among all nations.

In the background of this understanding of the classical city, there remains operative an ontology of fate and power. This precludes any perception of the universe that could justify a nonviolent or nondomination-oriented pattern of human behavior. The general spirit remains "imperial." Consequently, the public sphere is not a platform for a plurality of free associations but is itself an all-encompassing association. So public life consists of individual citizens or of family groups, but not of free associations.

The moral horizon in the West was redrawn by Christianity. This gave rise to a new type of civility, which could be described as a compromise between a transcendent vision and a reticent, immanent world. The new community envisioned by St. Paul had its citizenship in heaven. This, on principle, did not imply a withdrawal from this world but a new way of living in it and of obeying a new law, not the law of power and glory but the law of *agape,* love. In light of this transcendent vision, the classical civil morality and its concomitant public sphere were found wanting. Over against the ethos of pride, honor, and civil courage, the emerging Christian ethic concentrated on the notion of *agape* and denial of self. Worldly glory is vainglory, *vanitas.* Doing good is not intended to be visible to others, but only to God. Being a

Christian then entails a mental exodus from the classical *do ut des* scheme—give in order to receive—toward a scheme basically inspired by divine grace: *do quia mihi datum est*—I can give because much has been given to me.

Beneficence (*euergeteia*), or what we would term "philanthropy," is now meant to be hidden, a private act, rather than a public display. But it is public in the sense that its beneficiaries are not confined to an inner, private circle but are found on the streets, in the naked public square, along the roads; they are those who are in need for whatever reason. So the private act requires public presence: for example, buildings are built or bought to serve as shelter houses for the disabled, the homeless, the poor, the orphaned, or those in need of education.

Furthermore, as the philosopher at the Free University of Amsterdam, Govert Buijs, has argued, this precarious construction gave rise to a type of community that at first sight might be thought of as "uncivil"—the monasteries. But even the contemplative orders perceived themselves as existing for the well-being of all. Moreover, they embodied a new sense of the dignity of human labor, which had been despised in antiquity but now was recognized as an essential part of the human condition. *Ora et labora* (pray and work) was St. Benedict's dictum. And even a purely hermetic monk such as St. Pambo refused to eat anything for which he had not previously worked.

However, Christianity really entered the civil sphere in the establishment of the medieval cities of northern Italy and especially northwestern Europe. These cities could be called an experiment in Christian civility. The exodus from the bondage of feudalism turned out to be a societal experiment of world-historical significance. The city is a worldly though not at all a secular community. Out of an explicitly Christian inspiration the medieval cities realized what could be called a Western value coalition of free participation, social justice, and care for the weak—three key elements of many contemporary accounts of civil society. Moreover, we find here a keen sense of a differentiated social structure, in which different human activities are given their own institutional settings, in guilds, religious orders, lay orders, hospitals and orphanages, and what came to be known as universities, places of higher learning.

Thus we must take issue with a *genre* of interpretations of Christianity often inspired by German pietism and later by various forms of Marxism that treat Christianity as entirely otherworldly. These interpretations tend to overlook the impact of Christianity, exactly because it had the duality of otherworldliness and this-worldliness, even in its more contemplative expressions.

Crucial for the proper functioning of this value coalition was the ever-present possibility of experiencing both guilt and forgiveness. It served as a constant reminder of the fallibility and the temporal character of the civil experiment. It safeguarded both on an individual level and a collective level civil society's nonutopian character, for as soon as the awareness of imperfection and self-limitation erodes, the civil experiment is in jeopardy. It becomes vulnerable to various absolute threats, either the temptation to view the accumulation of wealth as the central goal of the civil experiment or the temptation to create an even better, more perfect world. So the efforts to establish civil societies are threatened by new absolute powers: state absolutism, religious fanaticism, and market possessiveness.

As a consequence, we should interpret the quest for the development of civil society in our day as a protest movement against the disparity, the ominous divide between the moral aspirations of Western culture on the one hand and the actual developments of society at large, particularly those of politics and economics, on the other hand. Neither the sovereign state with its *raison d'etat,* reasons of state, nor a totally sovereign economy, with its invisible-hand mechanism, seems to qualify as an embodiment of civil hopes as they had been articulated in medieval times.

Is this European tradition on its last legs? Has Europe run its course, now sinking into decay and decline? *Ich bin ein Europaïscher,* as President Kennedy might have put it. So, it is with a deep sense of disappointment and true sadness that I have to admit that *Europe is dying.* Europe's churches are empty. Masses on Sundays, in Gothic cathedrals and in small chapels, all across Europe, are virtually unattended. Not just sparsely filled—they are, except for a handful of tourists, vacant. Mass is typically now being conducted in a side chapel fit for the two dozen worshipers, mostly older women, who show up for it. Europe is adrift without a soul and evolving rapidly away from its moorings.

These glorious historic cathedrals are hardly the exception. Most of Europe's churches are unused these days, reduced to monuments for foreign tourists and artists to admire. And there is a reason for this neglect. In his controversial 2005 book, *The Cube and the Cathedral,* George Weigel, the biographer of Pope John Paul II, describes a European culture that has become not only increasingly secular but in many cases downright hostile to Christianity.[7] The cathedral in his title is Notre Dame, now overshadowed in cultural importance by the Arc de la Defense, the ultra-modernist "cube" that dominates an office complex outside Paris. "European man has convinced himself that in order to be modern and free, he must be radically secular," Weigel writes. "That conviction and its public consequences are at the root of Europe's contemporary crisis of civilizational morale."

It is true that throngs of believers recently descended on Rome to bid farewell to Pope John Paul II. And yet even as Catholics mourned the Pope's passing, Socialists and Greens in France decried the French government's decision to fly the flag at half-mast in his honor. Officials were reduced to claiming, in response, that the honor was afforded to John Paul in his capacity as a head of state, *not* as a religious leader.

The incident that forms the centerpiece of this critique is the recent debate over whether Christianity should be explicitly acknowledged in the European Union's constitutional treaty. By the time the draft constitution was completed in June 2004, a grudging reference to "the cultural, religious, and humanist inheritance of Europe" had been shoehorned into the preamble's first clause. This was about as much religion as Europe could stomach in a constitution that runs to some 70,000 words.

Practicing Christianity in Europe today enjoys a status not dissimilar to smoking marijuana or engaging in unorthodox sexual activities—few people mind if you do so in private, but you are expected not to talk about it much or ask others whether they do it too. Christianity is considered at best retrograde and atavistic in a self-described "progressive" society devoted to obtaining the good material life—long holidays, short work hours, and generous government benefits.

What is the deeper source of European antipathy to religion? For Weigel, the problem goes all the way back to the fourteenth century, when scholastics such as William of Ockham argued for nominalism. According to its philosophy, universals—concepts such as justice or freedom and qualities such as good—do not exist in the abstract but are merely words that denote instances of what they describe. A current of thought was set into motion, Weigel among others believes, that pulled European man away from transcendent truths. One casualty was any fixed idea of human nature.

If there is no such thing as human nature, then there are no universal moral principles that can be read from human nature. If there are no universal moral truths, then religion, positing them, is merely a form of oppression or functional myth, one from which Europe's elites see themselves as now liberated. And they look down on their American and third-world cousins who continue to believe in such irrational flights of fancy.

This is a big argument, and much more could be said to make it wholly convincing. One place to go for a fuller discussion is Richard Weaver's classic *Ideas Have Consequences*. In that seminal work he said, "The issue ultimately involved is whether there is a course of truth higher than, and independent of, man," He continued: "and the answer to the question is decisive for one's view of the nature and destiny of humankind."[8]

I think the critics are on firm ground when they analyze Europe's present condition, with its low birth rates, heavy government debts, Muslim immigration worries, and tendency to carp from the sidelines when the fate of nations is at stake. In what is certainly the most attention-grabbing passage in an engagingly written book, Weigel sketches the worst-case scenario, the "bitter end" for a Europe that is religiously bereft, demographically moribund, and morally without a compass: "The muezzin summons the faithful to prayer from the central loggia of St. Peter's in Rome, while Notre-Dame has been transformed into Hagia Sophia on the Seine—a great Christian church become an Islamic museum."

One need not find this scenario altogether plausible to feel persuaded by more measured arguments about Europe's atheistic humanism. Without a religious or spiritual dimension, a commitment to human freedom is likely to be attenuated, too weak to make sacrifices in its name. Europe's political elites especially, but its citizens as well, believe in freedom and democracy, of course, but they are reluctant to put the good life on hold and put lives on the line when freedom is in need of a champion—be it in the Balkans, the Sudan, Darfur, or, particularly, Iraq.

The good of human freedom, by European lights, must be weighed against the risk and cost of actually fighting for it. It is no longer transcendent, absolute. In such a world, governed by a narrow utilitarian calculus, sacrifice is rare, churches go unattended, and over time the spiritual capital that brought forth all that we know as the West is at risk of being *lost*. European society is much more post-materialist than North America, and its sense of thrift—of the need to sacrifice instant rewards for long-term benefits—is also gone.

I do not want to leave you with too pessimistic an account, which may nonetheless be accurate. So let me name five ideas that might turn the tables and perhaps, even begin to, if I was so bold to suggest, *revive* Europe: first, coming to grips with its unique place in world history and renewing the importance and source of those original ideals; second, some comprehension that *culture matters* and that Europe's culture has been the most formative for Western-Christian civilization— what used to be termed Christendom; third, accepting the social, political, economic, and especially military responsibility of a great continent, now more and more united; fourth, realizing the too evident demographic realities and Islamization and stepping up to reverse them so as to avoid an eventual Eurabia; fifth and most critical in my estimation, sparking a second great Reformation, spiritually, such that there is a wider recognition of transcendence and a moving of the spirit of God across the whole continent from the westernmost shores of Portugal, Ireland, and Britain to the easternmost steppes of Russia.

More than a few commentators suggest that Europe is a society adrift, untied from the source of its greatness; the very cultural foundation that provided the values making Europe great is disintegrating, leaving Europe (and soon the entire West) on sinking sand. More specifically, as the past is erased, rewritten, or ignored, the rich Judeo-Christian history of Europe is being left behind. And at what cost? The economic consequences are strong, but the cultural and political consequences are even more dire.

Weigel asks provocative questions. Why is European productivity dwindling to an all-time low? Why is European politics rife with senselessness? Why does Sweden have a considerably higher level of its population living below the poverty line? Why is Europe undergoing the "greatest sustained reduction in European population since the Black Death of the 14th century?" Could the recent woes of Europe be tied to the ever-decreasing Christian minority on this now decidedly post-Christian continent?

As I ponder this thesis of demise I am reminded of George Orwell's quote: "We have now sunk to a depth at which restatement of the obvious is the first duty of intelligent men." Weigel restates the obvious: "culture determines civilization." And he goes on to say that without its distinctly Christian history, Europe would not be what it is. Unfortunately, he may have more accurately written: "Europe would not have been what it *was*."

However, from the perspective of our Western tradition there is more to lament than the secondary effects of a decline in productivity, living standards, and art. Reviving religion as an end in itself is not what Europe needs. Quite the contrary, what it most seeks is rather a *call* back to its first love. Our modern theories and institutions, in Europe and America, are in peril today because they are not renewing themselves. History is replete with examples that tell us that it is great intellectual concepts in the realm of social, spiritual, artistic, and political reality that truly shape our destiny. We need to (re)focus the modern mind and the modern project, its theories and institutions, on the most important questions, the *perennial* questions, that face our nation, Europe, and the world. The place to turn to is the virtues; an ethics based on virtues would revive the ancient conversations we seem to have jettisoned as well as the Great Books and allow us again to consider the place of thrift in our personal, civic, and public lives.

## CHAPTER SEVEN

# Thrift and the Other Virtues

*"The thrift that does not make a man charitable sours into avarice. "*
— M.W. Harrison

Thrift and temperance are arguably among the central virtues, and they revolve in an orbit of many related virtues. But what generates virtues in the first place? In the words of St. Augustine: *Ego in hoc natus sum, et ad hoc veni ut veritatem attesti* [For this was I born, and for this I came into the world: to bear witness to the truth]. Does anyone attest to anything any longer? Are beliefs, or consensus on what is virtuous, more than subjective and relative? Do you believe in magic? How about Mother Nature? Do you believe that following *Cosmopolitan* or *Gourmet* or some other lifestyle magazine leads to the good life? Or that "the Nike *swoos*" is the mark of having arrived? Well, for the more affluent, how about a Rolex or BMW? Do you believe that being secure is synonymous with possessing superior physical power? Do you believe, as their advertisements suggest, that Nissan cars *save*—not gas or money but that they actually impart salvific value, as their advertising suggests? How would you counter the various forms of *unbelief*, or is there such a condition? Is there a theology of thrift? Unbelief includes:

- Heresy—the slide toward rationalism;

- Naturalism—the negation of revelation;

- Deism—which accepts only a limited mechanical God-cum-clockmaker? and,

- Atheism—the total denial of the supernatural?

Or do you even believe in *unbelief*?

Could you confront someone as brilliant as the late British philosopher and mathematical logician, Bertrand Russell, who not only refused to believe but also presented cogent arguments for *Why I Am Not A Christian*? Who leaves no room for virtue ethics and bases his ethics on the situation at hand?

Can you talk with person(s) who don't necessarily believe or disbelieve but are *indifferent* to your "damn" beliefs? What would you have to talk about, to find as common ground for agreement? Could you persuade, convince, or motivate such individuals? On what basis? Employing what apologetics? Which virtues? Applying whose interpretive hermeneutics over which agreed (sacred) texts? I want to try here to resolve two basic questions: First, what does it mean to believe? Second, what difference does it make? Belief and virtue are after all tied together.

These two questions should not and really cannot be separated. It is a mistake of post-Enlightenment Western philosophy and politics that allows us to even consider breaking them apart. For as the *ancients* knew, the practical tests of "abiding in God" are doctrinal as well as ethical. In other words, knowing God means demonstrating one's life by loving your neighbor and keeping God's commandments. It also implies assenting to a creed. Creeds of belief are nothing more than the Latin word *credo* suggests:

> brief authoritative summaries of the articles of faith—*your* faith. They are accepted and not necessarily seen. Divine mysteries. First causes.

The creed of I John 4:2 is both short and specific: "Jesus Christ has come in the flesh." Remember that belief itself is not a characteristic peculiar to religious folk. If that were the case, other people would lack belief altogether. Rather, belief is an essential part of the structure of our being human. Certain astute social scientists, such as Robert Lane at Yale, recognized this in their studies of core belief systems and human personality.[1] Lane suggested that the content and the direction of belief differ with people and cultures, and change along the long sweep of history.

Why do people believe? Why do you? Does anyone believe in the first place? Robert Lane, in his some 12 books on the subject of belief, suggested that people believe because they seek answers, answers about:

- the self, identity, and origin;
- the world, others, human nature, and relations;
- authority, appropriate behavior, legitimacy, and social structures;
- desires, wants, needs, motives, and goals;

- moral good, ethical behavior, and desire;
- explanatory systems, causation, and inference;
- time, place, and the order of things; and finally,
- concepts of knowledge, truth, and evidence.

These *core* belief systems guide our thought and action, be it economic, political, scientific, or religious—in any area of life. Beliefs are then perspectival, relational, and directive. They serve their proper purpose when they supply answers to the age-old, often called big questions:

- "What is real" (Metaphysics)
- "What is true" (Epistemology)
- "What is good" (Ethics)
- "What is beautiful" (Aesthetics).

In I John 5:20 we read that, "The Son of God has come." Do you believe this? It is worth noting that Jesus, the Christ, was called the only Son of God in the New Testament and the "I am" of the Torah or Old Testament. Very God, of very God.

A Messiah had long been expected. People had sought for many Saviors in whom to believe. Here we have what claims to be the most cataclysmic event of all time and interstellar space taking place in a backwater of the Roman empire in some provincial podunk of a town, born in a lowly manger, to a teenage, unwed Jewish girl of no status or wealth. God's choice for entering history is peculiar. As the historian Arnold Toynbee puts it, it is *His Story*, and as such, it became the turning point for all other human events. It became the axis on which everything else turns. Do you believe this story? Is this the best that God could do? How could it possibly be true? What are the implications?

When it comes to belief, there are only two basic choices for human persons. Belief can be directed toward God or toward an idol. We read in Exodus 20, Amos 5, Hosea 4, and Isaiah 40, among others, to *beware* of false gods, in other words, of false beliefs. The prohibition against serving other gods and the prohibition against making idols or images were already linked in the Decalogue itself. In fact, the entire prophetic message to Israel was that the misfortune that had overtaken the people was God's punishment for falling away from *Yahweh* and compromising their beliefs. The Jewish *shema* states it plainly, "Hear O Israel, the Lord my God is One." He is the only God, *ergo*—monotheism. It is important to recognize that in the New Testament the call to repentance always combined a demand for righteous behavior toward one's neighbor with the turning away from false gods.

Nineteen hundred years later in czarist Russia, Dostoyevsky's dreadful conclusion, which evolved with increasing conviction, was that without belief in God there is no hope for humanity and the world. Without God, he wrote, "anything would be permissible...and no law would have force." He concluded that there would be no purpose in life, no higher ideal, no aspiration for perfection, no sense of morality, and thus no discrimination between good and evil. Instead of a stream of progress, Dostoyevsky predicted

that humankind would "self-destruct" in a world consumed
by greed, self-centeredness, and exploitive gratifications of
the moment, truly becoming hell on earth. For him, man's
insatiable hunger is for God.

Presently, idols take *many* forms. Drugs, sex, and rock
and roll—these are perhaps the most familiar, at least in our
youth culture. Admittedly, our upwardly mobile adult idols
also include the contemporary sacred cows: wealth, health,
status, race, and power, among others. What do you worship? Are these much different from the two idols St. John
wrote about in his epistles to the first-century churches,
namely: Gnosticism, denying that Jesus Christ had come in
the flesh or that Jesus was divine; and, Doceticism, denying
the reality of Christ's human nature and his real suffering?

These "old heresies" pop up again and again in new
and novel forms in *modernity*. We call them by new names,
such as communism and socialism or some other *ism*. All
of these patently secular ideologies try to immanentize the
eschaton by bringing heaven to earth through revolution or
material prosperity, and in so doing each denies the transcendence of God.

Any *ism* represents an absolutization of a truth made
into a human idol, and as such it breaks both the first and
the fourth commandments, *that you shall have no other Gods
before me* and *that thou shall make no graven images in my like-
ness*. Apparently, our God is a jealous God and He demands
nothing short of *all* our devotion.

We read in Isaiah 45 where the power of Yahweh, who
molds history, is contrasted with the cult of idol worship,
"Woe to him who says, 'What are you begetting?'...Thus says

the Lord, I, I made the earth and created man upon it. It was my hands that stretched out the heavens, and I command all their hosts. I make straight all your ways." *Beware!* This God of Israel is strong, stronger than the idols St. John talks about, those lesser gods constructed out of human speculation; those lesser gods who do not give life; those lesser gods who are substitutes for the truth; those lesser gods of short-term gratification and deceit.

What should we believe? We hear incessant demands for values, family values, and values clarification. But the real question, the deeper one is, *which values?* Is one belief or set of values as good as any other? Was the positivist philosopher A. J. Ayer correct, that about all we can say about values is to utter statements like "vanilla ice cream is good," meaning merely, "I like vanilla ice cream"? Does the fashionable relativism imply that *any* preference is just as good as any other?

As for the content of faith, the orthodox confession "I believe in God" has its counterpart in the perennial secular confession "There is no God." In reality Sartre's statement "Life ends with death" is no less a profound confession of belief than "I believe in the resurrection of the dead."

What then do those in the Christian or Western tradition understand when they say the words "I believe"? Is it a nebulous, kind of wishy-washy undefined vagueness? A Kierkegaardian *leap* into, or is it from, darkness? So what, take it as you like, pick and choose: I'll have the easy version? Cheap grace? Is it just so much sentimentality—cute at Christmas and Easter and grudgingly acceptable at weddings and funerals? Or is it hard-nosed empiricism: I believe only what I can see, hear, touch, smell, and taste, sometimes referred to as "doubting Thomism"?

I suggest to you that there is no genuine belief, no matter how far away from the truth it may have fallen, that is not related to divine revelation; that *all* truth is God's truth. That is, I suspect, an audacious if not an outrageous statement to make, at the outset of the twenty-first century, the third millennium A.D. Which, by the way, still stands for "after the decension" of that Nazarene who claimed to be both God and man, fully divine and fully human. Even our calendars revolve around His life and death.

Belief is the kernel of meaning; is the ultimate assurance in time concerning the firm ground of your life, arising from a revelation of God as the origin of all things. The belief of which the biblical record speaks *grips* you in the heart of your existence. It saves you (unlike Nissan) in order to put you to work for some larger Kingdom purpose. As we read in Proverbs 4:23: "Above all else, guard your heart, for it is the wellspring of life." This is why Augustine, before he was ever a Saint, said in his *Confessions*, "I had first to believe in order to understand." Belief precedes action, and also, as Pascal opined, it always anticipates knowledge.

The spiritual direction of our hearts (the center of our being in the *ancient* Hebraic language), out of which emerge the issues of life, determines the shape of our entire system of belief. This is crucial! St. John is saying the very same thing in I John 5:6-7, which epitomizes Jesus's entire life and ministry: "This is He who came by water (i.e., his baptism) and blood (i.e., his death), Jesus Christ…And the Spirit is the witness because the Spirit is <u>the</u> Truth." In a powerful and bold treatment titled *The New Testament Speaks,* the Princeton theologian J. Ramsey Michaels suggests that here, in these few words, the gospel is reduced to its bare essentials: the ministry of Jesus from his baptism to his death upon the cross, revealed and interpreted by the Holy Spirit of truth. Believe it and have life, deny it and prepare for death.

Man cannot blaspheme and insult God and pay no penalty for *disbelief.* God is no liar! Everything hinges on believing—all knowledge, all joy, all meaning. The Church, following Christ's instruction, has taken this matter so seriously as to permanently memorialize the Lord's baptism and His death in the two sacraments of baptism with water and through the blood of the communion cup. These sacraments of belief have great evidential value. The Eucharistic action, through every generation since the first, is the most impressive and historic testimony of belief.

I was once told by an old Anglican missionary that each Christian convert in his diocese of North India was taught to put their hand on their head every morning to remind themselves of their baptism and to repeat the words, "Woe to me if I preach and live not the gospel." By better understanding the nature of belief, we must press the urgent question: What difference does comprehension of the Christ event make? If we take the gospel accounts seriously, there are two significant differences in the lives of believers. The first has to do with something we have trivialized, called love. The second involves a very old-fashioned word, righteousness. "Love," or *agape* in Greek, not *eros*, is literally caring for your neighbor. Simply put, when you do not love your neighbor, you do not know God.

The most disastrous error in the history of Christianity (under the influence of Stoic Greek philosophy, nonetheless in the second century) was to differentiate love and justice. It cannot be done! I think John 3:17-18 is clear on this: "If anyone has material possessions and sees his brother in need but has no pity on him, how can the love of God be in him? Dear children, let us not love with words or tongue but with actions and in truth." Equally clear is the word of the prophet in Jeremiah 22:16, "He defended the cause of the poor and needy, and so all went well. Is that not what it means to know me?" declares the Lord.

With great intuition a twentieth-century Latin American theologian from Argentina pointed this out in modern language when he penned: "The supreme delicacy of charity is to recognize the right of the person being given to, because of this recognition, love is love and not a humiliating paternalism." "Righteousness," on the other hand, is *not* as Socrates *à la* Plato would have it, a matter of actions conforming to a given set of autonomous, man-made, self-enlightened, rational legal standards. It is proper behavior in obedient service to God. God's righteous acts are redemption and salvation, and man's response in the covenant is keeping His commands. Doing right and walking humbly before the Lord has been best memorialized in the powerful and moving old black spirituals.

This relationship depends on God's gift, but it calls for a corresponding goodness in the personal and collective lives of the people He asks us to follow Him. Paul used the term "righteous" more frequently than any other New Testament author, and he meant by it God's dealings with

His people, the new humanity. Belief in the one man Christ defies the curse of sin and brings to the world new possibilities. The gospel proclaims boldly, "In Christ behold all things become new." In I John 5:4-5 we read, "This is the victory which has overcome the world: our faith. Who overcomes the world but he who believes that Jesus is the Son of God?" The power of belief should never be underestimated. There is nothing, absolutely no thing that the world fears so much as our being convinced that the Kingdom of God has and will come.

To the extent that we realize that Jesus is the Messiah, the Kingdom of God is achieved. The outcry of the oppressed ceases, and we overcome the world—not as this is usually interpreted as if the gospel were a series of ascetic contests or an inward journey of subjectivism or new age *hocus pocus* with mere individual importance. Rather, belief in Christ is about human freedom; it is about doing justice. The gospel, which itself means "good news," is about man's *response* to God's story, about the faithful, obedient, stewardly cultural formation of His followers. Read Romans 5. All of the four gospels insist on precisely the same thing. Paul sums it up in a single sentence: "Everything which does not stem from faith is sin."

Christianity is not a matter of expediency, some long-term Faustian bargain of hedonism in a happy afterlife. It is either recognition of the rule of God over all of life—where we live—or it is utterly meaningless. Too often it has become at best a trapping or the vestige of some past time, relevant only to more primitive peoples or the medieval monasteries.

No! There is a war to wage right here. And this battle is I think perhaps most graphically portrayed in the movie *Chariots of Fire*. The protagonist, a Scottish Calvinist, Eric Liddell, explains in one scene why he runs and why he so diligently prepared for the 1924 Paris Olympics. He and his sister, Jennie, are at *Arthur's Seat*, a marvelous hill overlooking the magical capital city of Edinburgh. Eric says to her, "I believe that God made me for a purpose. But he also made me *fast*. And when I run, I feel His pleasure. I run to honor God." His sibling's response, "Then run in God's name and let the world stand back in wonder," is a testament to how God uses his followers. Not only did Eric Liddell win the gold medal in the 1000 meters, a race for which he did not train, but he also was a sprinter who would not run the dash on the Sabbath. He became a renowned missionary who later died in China. Evil and banality have won much since then; perhaps some of us prefer *Chariots* as much as we do for its vivid evocation of a simpler and more innocent age. Corruption and modernity (especially in the form of the Olympic Committee) are easily won over; beauty is never uncoupled from virtue; and nobility is unfailingly and gracefully noble.

So, you may rightly ask, "how" can anyone, a college student, a busy teacher, a businessperson, *believe*, legitimately believe, in the face of hunger, nuclear and other holocausts, AIDS, genocide, murder, the degradation of our environment, sickness, terrorism, or staring at death itself? My humble reply: Try to fathom the meaning of the Lord's Prayer by comparing what Christ taught us to say with what it means in our lives today. That Kingdom will come on earth, and His will be done, just as fully as it is now in heaven. The prayer He taught His disciples for the coming of that Kingdom demands that you and I struggle on its behalf in the whole order of creation: Believe in the truth, *and run*.

Have confidence in God; call on His name. Have communion with the Father, and the Son, and the Holy Spirit. Do justice and *believe* the promise of God's word that "we are in Him who is true, in His Son Jesus Christ. This is the true God and eternal life." As you think, study, struggle, suffer, and find joy in this life, you will see how God is working His purposes out...from age to age, in your own life, in your own family, in your school, in your government, and in the world, at large. Take hold, rejoice and be glad, give thanks and *run* because eternal life has already begun for those that only *believe*.

I have argued that out of belief issues forth virtue or excellent moral reasoning and behavior. The debate over which virtues, their priority, and the nature of virtues needs to be rejoined. Kenneth Minogue, a political philosopher, has articulated a sound argument about the need for the re-introduction of virtue ethics.[2] He thinks that prudence is the virtue that guides us through the dangers that threaten life, fortune, and integrity. Many of these dangers come from outside us, but all of them ultimately stem from our own weakness, which is the reason why prudence is a virtue—that is to say, an overcoming of temptation. But as with all virtues, temptations are ambiguous. When we construe all our impulses as temptations to be controlled we may not be living the highest form of the moral life. It may not always be prudent to expend one's capital in generous acts, for example, but it may well be admirable. For this reason, prudence is a virtue whose ambiguity makes it interesting, even though it too is currently out of fashion.

Part of the reason prudence, like thrift, features little in current moral thinking is that we are now casual in our understanding of the moral life. We don't hear many sermons and expect to be bored if we do. The priest, rabbi, or clergyman has given way to the nonjudgmental counselor, and any standard schedule of virtues is treated with suspicion. We don't much concern ourselves with a moral plan of life or a set of principles, for our basic stance is that we are all competent to make our own moral decisions and indeed have a duty to do so. We take our moral cues from the changing circumstances of life, from the changing journalism we read and television we watch, and from what the people around us, our peers, are saying. This does not mean that we are altogether morally insouciant: Some people are indeed pretty hand to mouth about their obligations, but many people live lives of constant moral confusion. But all can recognize imprudence in such forms as unwanted pregnancy or unmanageable debt. Today, prudence is largely risk avoidance, rather than the orchestrator of our virtues, as it used to be in earlier times. This is a new situation, and to understand it we must remember that prudence, like other virtues, has a history, so its significance has never been entirely stable.

Among the classical Greeks, *phronesis* referred to practical wisdom and in particular the skill of managing cities. Prudence is one possible translation of *phronesis,* and even among the Greeks it could also refer to the skill of managing one's individual life.

The core meaning of virtue is excellence, and moral virtue is moral excellence. What we admire is a human being choosing to be courageous, generous, candid, and so on, in circumstances where many people would be tempted to behave badly. All the virtues are excellences, but can we say that a person who exhibits all the virtues is a moral paragon, a perfect person? Given the imperfections of human life, of course, we may say that this would in practice be impossible, but there is a much more significant problem: The virtues cannot add up to the single coherent excellence because they contain internal contradictions. Different occupations—such as that of doctor or priest—have their own specific excellences, and those will sometimes conflict with other virtues. In the first book of the *Republic* Plato explores the virtues found in a robber band, but these, like all occupationally based forms of excellence, are not adequate to and are sometimes directly in conflict with what a real human community must have. How amid all this conflict can we find the good itself, that quality in terms of which all virtues are a form of moral excellence?

If we could find it, this would be the moral philosopher's stone, but we have not found it yet, and it seems unlikely that we shall be able to do so. In the modern state different "moralities" are in conflict, and our admiration for one virtue will often be at odds with our admiration for another. What makes the courageous warrior admirable may well be despised by the saintly and the peace-loving. The responsibilities of the statesman may at times require (as Machiavelli insisted) vice rather than virtue; indeed, sometimes vice may be *virtu*. The confidentiality of the professional may conflict with the safety of the state. An important reason for the incoherence of our system of virtues results from the fact that we have acquired these admirations over a long period of time. We inherited from the classical world the pagan virtues of wisdom, temperance, courage, and justice, but Christianity soon supplemented them with, or perhaps infiltrated into them, such virtues as faith, hope, and charity. It is hardly too much to say that each generation has its favorite virtues jostling in a system that is seldom at rest. How then may the moral agent, whose broad aim is to do the right thing, navigate a way through these indeterminacies?

We may reformulate the problem by observing that virtues and vices are the names of abstract qualities, which means that understanding their character depends significantly on the context in which they occur. To every virtue, in fact, there corresponds a vice that results from its foolish implementation. The generous man should not become a spendthrift or the courageous man rash; the teller of truth ought not to become a "candid friend" or tactless character. On the wall of Southwark Cathedral in London can be found commendation for a chaplain who was "pious without ostentation" and "zealous with discretion." Every structure of virtues, then, needs some higher-level guidance about how to balance our conduct. This guidance may function in two logically distinct ways, one intellectual and the other practical.

Philosophically, the virtues will be found to reveal some underlying form of intellectual organization that in a sense might explain their virtuous character. Aristotle, for example, thought that moderation was not only a virtue in itself but also in a sense the "orchestrator" or "architectonics" of all the virtues. We have no such lead virtue today and are at a loss for it.

What remains, then, of the virtue of prudence? All those governmental agencies are so good to us, and spread their benefits so widely, that it might be thought that the modern state had quite abolished any need for prudence. But the entire abolition of prudence would require that the burden of individual self-consciousness, that famous fall in the Garden of Eden, when we realized that we needed a fig leaf, should at last be taken from us. Some radical utopians, such as Plato, have indeed dreamed of just this. Poor Winston Smith in Orwell's *1984* lived in a society of this kind, and it was based on the idea that such self-consciousness was the root of all evil. Both money and private property were thought, rightly, to flow from it. But it is hard to imagine a human being lacking this interesting dimension of consciousness. The philosopher Thomas Hobbes in *Leviathan* argued that the greatest pleasure for human beings was superiority, and while the state can try to abolish the prudence that in some degree curtails this drive, it cannot abolish the propensity to think of oneself advantageously. Prudence no doubt will have to change its character, but being the tame lion among the virtues, it will.

Last year at Stanford University, Apple Computer CEO Steve Jobs gave a short graduation address that became instantly famous and was circulated widely on the Internet.[3]

He told three deeply personal stories and concluded: You need to connect the dots, by staying young and staying foolish. I recommend his *hip* speech to you but do not think its recommendations (hardly virtues) nearly sage enough.

In a similar vein, I have three stories to close out this chapter. Max Dupree, the wise CEO of the Fortune 500 furniture company Herman Miller, Inc., who was also a college and seminary president, it could be added, says in his book *Leadership Jazz*, "Pointing the way and saying thank you is the first and last word of true leadership."[4] Remember that good advice. Being nice, polite, and grateful is no more difficult than the opposite. In fact, doing so pays large rewards. In the Bible we were told to have a joyful heart; how do we get one? It starts with praise and thanksgiving, goes through forgiveness, and leads directly to service leadership; these traits are cause and effect.

Here, then, are my three short (moral) stories. The first one took place in Europe nearly five hundred years ago; it involved *our* ancestors in the Protestant Reformation. Both Luther and Calvin used the word "vocation" or "calling," from *Berufung* in German, with reference to someone calling or addressing one, *vocally*. The one who called was the living God. Their view was different from the prevailing medieval sense of a restricted calling of a person to leave his/her work and enter a monastic way of life or holy office. The Reformers held that Christ's crucifixion and resurrection from the dead was a total victory that included the salvation of both life and nature. Natural work was already sanctified and did not require prior or additional sanctification dispensed by a church or through sacraments. Since then, everywhere human beings stand and live *Coram Deo*, directly before the face of the living God, who summons them to serve Him and their neighbors by doing *what* they do—as farmers, craftsmen, kings, housewives, or merchants. Daily work itself became a vocation; it needed no further spiritual dimension.

Many have tied this concept of work to the emerging doctrine of the sovereignty of God. It is critical for understanding the role of persons in the world. The question I put to you is this: Does this sovereignty relate to soteriology as well as individual salvation? Or has God's sovereignty been slowly shoved to the margins and effectively privatized? If linked to creation it has wide implication. The familiar biblical phrase "Christ is Lord of All" should mean more than lordship of narrow individual behavior or for one hour on Sunday morning in a church pew. The phrase has a cultural mandate, also impelling action in society and in the economy. The possibilities are manifold, all with an option to serve God or to bend to another manmade idol. Faithful stewardship is careful administration of what has been entrusted to you by someone higher than yourself. In Aristotle the *oeconomia*, which translates as "stewardship," did not have to do with some separate category of ethics that can or cannot be related to real-life decisions. It had to do with the whole character of the actor. We have today removed this normative element.

The question of this story of old is simply: What is your calling? Listen…even now for the quiet voice of Him who made and sustains you. You have to have the courage to pick up your nets and have the faith to *follow Him* wherever it takes you. If you need encouragement I suggest that you read N. T. Wright's little book, *Simply Christian*.[5] He supplies a focused view of the meaning of Easter: "When Jesus emerged from the tomb, justice, spirituality, relationship and beauty rose with him. Something happened in and through Jesus, as a result of which the world is a different place, a place where heaven and earth have been joined forever. God's future has arrived in the present."

While you may think you have finished your education or that you now possess a *terminal* degree, I have to tell you that nothing could be further from the truth. You see the global economy we compete in, and the very nature of free enterprise and competition means that you all will have to become what I call "perpetual learners," because the minute you stop learning you die. I do not want to leave you with an impression that this is just mad activity, memorizing more facts or cramming for more tests as cogs caught up in the hustle and bustle of modern life. The German philosopher Josef Pieper once wrote an elegant work that suggested that leisure is nothing less than "an attitude of mind and a condition of the soul that fosters a capacity to perceive the reality of the world."[6] He demonstrated that leisure has been, and always will be, the first foundation of any culture, and he observed that "in our bourgeois Western world total labor has too often vanquished leisure. Unless you regain the art of silence and insight, the ability for non-activity, unless you substitute true leisure for our hectic amusements, we will destroy our culture, its collected wisdom—and ourselves." So continue to set time apart for thinking, for praying, and for re-creation. Be perpetual learners!

My second story began a number of years ago on a beautiful and balmy spring day as we flew into the Bahamas and went through the gates of the private Lyford Cay Club. My heart raced, as I was about to encounter the world's greatest investor for the first time. I was not there, as so many before me had trekked, to gain some useful perspective on the market or to discover which global companies to invest in. My conversation was even more profound. Over time, I was privileged to have many conversations with him and to embark on a friendship that turned into a *challenge*.

Sir John Templeton came immediately across as a humble yet penetrating soul. His gaze was truly like that of a sage, of a person both entirely otherworldly and so infused with spiritual information that he exuded, well—*joy*. He enjoined me in a direct yet simple challenge—to demonstrate how enterprises and the entrepreneurs who started them are guided by a spiritual force rooted in faith. I took up his challenge and with his generous support and my own endowment, founded the Spiritual Enterprise Institute.

What challenges you? What do you want to be remembered for when all is said and done? Do not fall prey to the temptations of material life, of work as toil or living without a purpose. Make yours a purpose-driven life. Make a difference not just for yourself but also for something that lasts for eternity. It may not make you popular, rich, or famous—that was never promised. As C. S. Lewis put it in his tales of Narnia, captured now in film: "He doesn't like being tied down—of course he has other countries to attend to. It's quite all right. He often drops in. Only you mustn't press him. He's wild, you know. Aslan is not like a tame lion." Aided by that wise and magnificent lion, the children lead Narnia into a spectacular climactic battle to be free of the wicked witch's glacial powers forever!

You may have achieved a personal milepost, but rarely do you achieve results entirely from your own effort. You, like I, will or have been blessed in this life with loving parents, a helpful spouse, many friends, wonderful children, and a community of people, a network of colleagues and supporters, a free country, the list goes on and on—all who have both believed and invested in *you*. For this, be eternally grateful and fully acknowledge that *no* person is an island or formed of his/her own being. We are works in progress and are designed with meaning in it all. Purposes are being worked out throughout the ages, even here and now. Be willing to play your part in *His story*.

Neither is a life entirely one's own product. Rather, it is shaped by the tides of the times and one's own background, experiences, and mentors. Having been reared in an observant home and raised in the cradle of Reformed faith, I was never outside of belief. My intellectual pedigree, interdisciplinary training, and a life of real world work led me to undertake the tasks I have been given. As an academic, who early on became a "recovering academic," I was perhaps fortunate to leave the ivory tower to join the blood, sweat, and tears of the active life. Wherever I have been involved, in politics, investment banking, diplomacy, and for nearly the last two decades the corporate world, as a strategist, I have tried, often failed, and tried again to be a Christian. From Davos to Aspen I have had the good fortune to interact with and to come to know senior business people, keen on inventing the future. I have come to know them and their companies, and to advise them while peering into their souls. What have you been challenged to do? When people read your obituary 10, 20, 60, or 70 years hence, what will your lasting contribution be?

My final act: I grew up singing old *and* new hymns. The songs I most recall include the likes of *Hide It Under a Bushel, Yes, Jesus Loves Me, Deep and Wide,* and the classics from past eras. For me, faith was and remains the ultimate purpose for living and serving. Each summer my family would travel from the heat and humidity of the inner city to vacation at a camp in the Adirondack Mountains, on what is, literally, Lake Pleasant. The image still reverberates in my overeducated mind, especially on sleepless nights. It was as cool, calm, and refreshing a place as is a heavenly breeze. That is because it likely was. It was a religiously inspired but nondenominational setting. We were called *gospel volunteers*—as if we were free and roving ambassadors for Christ. I guess I still am. I recall my last summer there, then as a counselor. Every Sunday morning at chapel, set high on a hill overlooking that ever-pleasant lake, we would march in carrying about a hundred different flags. They were from nearly every country around the globe —from America to Zimbabwe. As the campers paraded forward to the stage, the orchestra would play and the ebullient choir would sing in the loudest and most melodious voices I have ever heard *Crown Him with Many Crowns… Thy praise and glory shall not fail for all eternity.*

My hope is that you readers will have your own Lake Pleasant, as a reservoir of strength, and that you will remember special places of higher education, brilliant mentors, spiritual guides, the character and friendships formed in life, so that you can give all the Glory to God. You need to locate your moral compass and arrange your virtues, including thrift, in order to live the good life. Because in the end, life is a calling, and taking on *your* challenge is nothing more than a long *doxology*: from Him all blessings flow and to Him they shall return. Since they are His and will be again, our thrifty use of these endowments or resources is, for the time we have care over them, another statement of our thrift as earthkeepers and earthbuilders.

## CHAPTER EIGHT

# Democratic Morality and Spiritual Enterprise

*"Beware of little expenses; a small leak will sink a great ship."*
—Benjamin Franklin

I have argued that economics cannot be separated from morals and character. Thrift, both public and private, is a core virtue. "Ordinary integrity," Edmund Burke wrote, "must be secured by the ordinary motives to integrity." Thrift, honesty, and ingenious effort are rewarded in economic life. For Burke, "the vast majority work principally out of self-interest, to benefit themselves and their families. There is nothing wrong with this state of affairs; it is merely a condition of ordinary human nature. Competition puts a premium on industry, thrift, honesty, and ingeniousness, for the slothful, the spendthrift, the known cheats, and the stupid fall behind in the economic contest of free enterprise."[1]

In the end, it is true that more than any specific values or virtues, it is the reluctance to speak the language of morality and to apply moral ideas to social policies that separates us more than anything else from the ancients and the virtuous Victorians. The Victorian virtues, rooted in the Protestant Reformation—work, thrift, temperance, respectability—are, as others have suggested, quite modest, even mundane. They rest on no special breeding, status, talent, wisdom, grace, or money. They are, in the ultimate sense, *democratic.*[2]

The Victorians have too often been condemned as materialist, racist, self-righteous, hypocritical, imperialist, and even, worst of all, earnest. Yet as Lytton Strachey's latest treatment *Eminent Victorians* now shows, these "sturdy, steadfast Britons confronted the most tumultuous challenges: the incredible rise of industrialism, the rapid spread of railroads, the shift from farm labor to work in mines and mills, the teeming swarm to city living, the soul-wrenching clash of new scientific ideas with ancient religious beliefs, and ultimately, the burden of empire."[3] The Victorian premium on the *self*—self-help, self-interest, self-control, self-respect, and self-discipline —allowed for a truly liberal society. It upheld the self, *not* selfishness, in the context of the family, the other mediating "little platoons," and the State. That society of middle-class adherents anchored in democratic capitalism believed in and required nothing less than a moral citizenry. Do not sell thrift short, for thrift, as a Victorian virtue with deep-seated Calvinist origins, has ultimately made possible *both* capitalism and democracy.

In *The Decline of Western Democracy,* Walter Lippmann, an American intellectual of unparallel greatness, remarked, "There has developed in this century a functional derangement of the relationship between the mass of the people and the government. The people have acquired power which they are incapable of exercising and the governments they elect have lost powers which they must recover if they are to govern."[4]

The unhappy truth is that the prevailing public opinion has been destructively wrong at the critical junctures. "The people have imposed a veto upon the judgments of informed and responsible officials. They have compelled the governments, which usually knew what would have been wiser ... Mass opinion has acquired mounting power in this century. It has shown itself to be a dangerous master. There have been men worth listening to who warned the people against their mistakes. Always, too, there have been men inside the governments who judged correctly because they were permitted to know in time the uncensored and unvarnished truth. But the climate of modern democracy does not usually inspire them to speak out."[5]

Lippmann thought the exceptions so rare "that they are regarded as miracles and freaks of nature; successful democratic politicians are insecure and intimidated men. They advance politically only as they placate, appease, bribe, seduce, bamboozle, or otherwise manage to manipulate the demanding and threatening elements in their constituencies. The decisive consideration is not whether the proposition is good but whether it is popular—not whether it will work well and prove itself but whether the active, talking constituents like it immediately. Politicians rationalize this servitude by saying that in a democracy public men are the servants of the people."[6]

What is the possible antidote? How do we move ahead while at the same time recovering our past? The answer I think lies in a model of what I call *spiritual capital*. If we can create more spiritual capital it will give rise to more enterprise or virtuous companies, which in turn will create yet more virtuous behavior, rooted in both culture and character in a continuous circle or feedback loop.

Spiritual capital is a form of capital that aligns with its cousins, both human capital and social capital, each of which has a long pedigree and an abundant literature. But it is also much more. It is the normative, directional dimension, which gives meaning and purpose to all human activity.

Spiritual capital has real and measurable economic value, especially in connection with entrepreneurship and the creation of both innovative products and services and the creation of prosperity. By invoking spiritual capital we complete the picture, demonstrating the conceptual linkages and relations of human and social capital and tying these forms of capital to core processes in the creation of prosperity. In spiritual capital wealth generation is paramount. Without the generation of wealth there would be no charity, services, or flourishing at all.

There are three possible models for the origins of prosperity: One, the sources of prosperity are *mysterious*, as in so many myths of origins, guarded by gnomes and spirits under the earth and reluctantly given to humans, who must use magic and trickery to gain access to them; two, prosperity grows through tribal, corporate, and national conquests that seize wealth from others; three, wealth is created by the exercise of human energies. The first two views assume that wealth is a pre-existing fixed resource that simply moves from one column to another in some hypothetical account book. The third view posits that prosperity is open, expandable, and can be created by human knowledge and effort. The theory of spiritual capital springs from this third way.

In other words, the concept of spiritual capital posits that the sources of prosperity are knowable and that prosperity can be spread by knowledge and education. This does not mean that spiritual capital is human to the point of excluding a transcendent point of reference or co-creator. The idea of spiritual capital is deeply rooted in natural law and the theological study of God's action in the world. At the same time, the concept has sufficient structure and integrity to define a set of human and social capacities that can operate independently of any theology or specific set of religious beliefs. Again, theology, and likely some theologies more than others, may provide the deepest conceptual base for a theory of spiritual capital, but the theory can be articulated on its own terms. For now, we will simply point to these issues without deeper examination.

The importance of the concept and its effect increases dramatically in the context of our emerging knowledge economy based on innovation. In the past, attention has focused on financial capital and physical capital as static, limited assets to be accumulated, invested, and managed. The source of economic prosperity was taken for granted, as an existing condition to be exploited. In this context, economics was modeled on the basis of resource management in large systems, with growth and development coming largely from the management of costs. Today, it is impossible to "cost cut" to prosperity; innovation is unleashing a new wave of economic disruption to major industrial systems;

and new interest is being focused on the very origins of prosperity. The concept of spiritual capital can help to shed light on this entrepreneurial feature of economic activity, which has often been left shrouded in mystery or simply taken for granted.

Spiritual capital is not simply the set that includes human and social capital. Nor is it a static quantity or asset, like money in the bank. It is a dynamic and complex cultural system that helps to create all the other forms of capital on which a workable economy depends. It is what some have referred to as the glue that makes everything stick together, or "moral ecology." Spiritual capital can also be understood as a type of code, like the genetic code, the grammar of a language, or the code for a computer program; from this perspective, spiritual capital is more narrowly defined in terms of embedded concepts and theories. It is embedded and transmitted principally at the level of tacit knowledge: the knowledge that informs our free choices and that tells us what to do at the moment of action.

A code is an underlying pattern that determines how a system will operate and change in relation to other systems and the environment over time. Some codes are closed and are used to replicate identical structures and functions every time. Other codes are open and self-organizing. Using matrix code levels to preserve core invariance through change, open codes interact with the environment and may themselves change and develop over time without collapsing or completely changing themselves at any one time. For example, the grammar of a language is hierarchical in this way, and this allows a language to change its grammar drastically over time without ever ceasing to be grammatical at any one time. The genetic code also uses a core alphabet and structure to create many various forms of life, and through those organisms and their reproductive fate the genetic code continues to develop.

Spiritual capital is very much like grammar or the genetic code in that it is open, self-organizing, and able to develop new forms over time. This self-organizing capacity, combined with the level distinctions among knowledge, personal behavior, and social structure, introduces a significant range of freedom into the system. As the genetic code for human and social capital, spiritual capital is built primarily though learning, the generation of knowledge, and the intellectual and spiritual practices that promote creative response and receptivity to novelty from outside any formal system of knowledge. As Kurt Gödel's Incompleteness Theorem shows, some truths exist outside any consistent set of axioms able to generate them. The growth of spiritual capital requires both intellectual capacities — the capacity to build and test propositional systems and formal models— and the capacity to "think outside the box" to be receptive to truths from outside the system and to new "paradigms."

This understanding also means that religious, scientific, academic, corporate, and educational institutions, together with the emerging smart technologies and the vast archives and data, are the primary contexts in which spiritual capital develops. That said, there are also important roles for government and private enterprise to play in relation to spiritual capital and its systems of knowledge. Today, new "translation platforms" need to be created that define social theories and models that engage spiritual capital formation in effective ways to the work of government, the social sector, and business. Defining these platforms and core concepts integral to optimal spiritual capital formation is an area ripe for serious scholarly research and development. It would serve as the foundation for broadening the base for prosperity and expanding the pursuit of happiness.

How can we proactively generate more spiritual capital if it is so critical? Michael Lindsay, an advisor on religion and culture for the Gallup Institute, recently reported on a major study of the state of spirituality in the United States.[7] Gallup, in conjunction with the Program for Research on Religion and Urban Civil Society at the University of Pennsylvania, produced an *Index* surveying the comparative strengths of "inner" and "outer" commitments to religious beliefs: 72% of Americans said their faith gave meaning and purpose to their lives. Americans are on a quest for spiritual wholeness, but this finding should not to be confused with a reaffirmation of specific doctrinal positions. Instead, Americans are looking for spiritual meaning in their lives, which may or may not be connected to one particular denominational tradition.  And 60% of Americans think that their faith is involved in every aspect of their lives, demonstrating that Americans want to integrate their faith commitments into the social, professional, and civic arenas as well.  Lindsay went on to describe the shape of that commitment. While a very close relationship with Jesus is important to evangelical Americans, they belong to the 60% of the American population who would turn to Jesus only in times of crisis. So, Lindsay concluded, there is an element professing very strong beliefs but often failing to put them into practice.   In the future, leaders can build upon Americans' burgeoning spiritual interests to produce deeper levels of commitment.

Some commentators have begun to offer empirical findings about the term and field of spiritual capital. One economist thought of Weber's definition and has wondered if one could draw parallels between economics and spirituality. The term "spiritual capital" suggests that some connection is being drawn between the transcendent spiritual world and materialistic economics. The issue at hand has to do with whether capital can be understood as an element of the spiritual side of life to help us better understand, analyze, and improve the material side. The concept of human capital, as has been noted, helps us to understand the economic contribution that labor makes to production. Thinking about human capital leads us to reflect on spiritual capital. Is there a self-adjusting feature in spiritual capital? Are there any incentives that would lead us to invest in more? What does spiritual capital produce that is important for the development of markets? Ideas? Morality? Does it reproduce itself? Can it be renewed? Is it possible to distinguish between different kinds of spiritual capital? Could we trade it? Can it be spent? Borrowed? Lent to others? Securitized?

It may not be in anyone's best interests to restrict an understanding of spiritual capital to an investigation of market incentives and profitable motivations. Material prosperity fosters humanitarian actions. Spiritual capital has the potential to build a bridge between the transcendent and material sides of human life and so lessen the destructive results of misunderstanding. What can be done with it? An opposing question is important to consider: What has spiritual capital gotten people not to do? It is not desirable to employ politics to attain all human goods. American forms of religion have inspired a sober attitude toward politics. Is there spiritual political capital? How is it manifested and how is it different from what has been termed civil religion?

Spiritual capital growing out of spiritual discipline and formed in virtuous behavior may provide partial or fuller answers and responses to these five crises besetting us:

- The *crisis in ethics* that besets us as a people and in almost all of cultural and professional life.

- The root causes of and spiritual basis for the current predicament in governance in business, the professions, and non-profits and government.

- A *way out*, which includes economic development that is transformative in nature and sustainable in principle, drawing on the multiplicity of religious traditions that make America great and in essence a "city on a hill" in the Augustinian sense.

- The role of religion and spirituality in domestic lives and in the faith of the President and in the nation-building as far away as Iraq and the Middle East.

- The crucial linkage between democracy, freedom, and capital.

Spiritual capital may in fact be the missing link to social and economic progress. Rodney Stark, professor at Baylor University and author of many titles on the subject, has declared that it is perfectly acceptable to celebrate Mammon.[8] He is interested in the socially beneficial effects of religious institutions—not only in terms of human benefits but also in terms of actual dollars. There is, he has maintained, a very substantial religious effect on crime, that is, religious people do less of it. Therefore, it can be assumed that if there was no spiritual capital, the crime rate would rise significantly. Costs to society would also rise, as more police, prisons, and parole officers would be required. If the private school system shut down because it was no longer able to receive funds form religiously motivated groups of people, it would cost the government billions of dollars to absorb the new students in the public system. Religious faith also has a significant effect on personal health. Measurements can be made in terms of the proportionally smaller use of drugs and alcohol among religious people. There is also a vast literature that has developed around the idea that religion positively affects a person's health. For a final example, one could venture to say that without a strong religious sentiment, there would be many more abandoned mothers and children than there are presently. All of these behaviors have large societal costs. Put another way, if there were no spiritual capital someone would have to pay for all these bad and costly behaviors.

Stark has been careful to note that one cannot assign an actual dollar value to spiritual capital. However, he argues that it can be measured in terms of happiness.

Cheerful Europeans, for example, are believing non-be-longers. Although they are not very faithful in attending church, they have faith and do pray regularly. Stark explains the unique European situation in terms of a lack of competition between different denominations. In Italy, however, there is a religious revival in the process. In five years Italy potentially could generate a lot of spiritual capital. Due to its religiosity, America currently has much spiritual capital. In conclusion, Stark ventures a rough but no doubt conservative estimate of the amount of money religion is saving the American taxpayer.

Robert Barro, the well-known professor of economics at Harvard University, has made some similar remarks in studies he and his colleagues have made on religious experience around the world, which for the first time have included data on Muslim countries.[9] He has shown that religion and culture are important social forces and are likely to matter when measuring economies. What are the determinants of religiosity? What are the determinants of economics? Contrary to Stark's position on state-sanctioned religions that are established, Barro demonstrates that the impact of having a state religion is generally positive on the level of religiosity in a country's population. The economic impact of religiosity can be measured. For example, a more intense belief in heaven and hell improves economic development. Barro interprets the empirical evidence as saying that eschatological beliefs cultivate the kind of character traits that further economic growth. Thrift is most certainly one of the key traits, and it leads directly to higher savings rates.

Barro distinguishes simple religiosity from a religiosity that encourages the regular attendance of churches. While religiosity provides a positive stimulus to the economy, too much church attendance could actually reduce the potential level of economic growth. Notably, the economic consequences of increased religiosity are negligible.

In a number of his books but most recently in *The Universal Hunger for Liberty*, Michael Novak has addressed the clash of civilizations thesis made popular by Samuel Huntington.[10] He has noted the differing Muslim and Christian perspectives on the concept of God's image. Muslims tend to say that human beings in no way can be made in the image of God, for God is entirely other. Christianity, on the other hand, sees humankind as created in the image of God and therefore to be responsible for certain tasks that God has given them—in essence to realize their innate potential as co-creators with God. Novak stresses the importance of recognizing a human *moral ecology*. He defines moral ecology as the sum of all those conditions, ideas, narratives, and civil arrangements with which human beings operate that help them to mature as moral beings. Democratic living, Novak has said, requires a limit to individual behavior' that must be assumed. He also sees that capitalism is much more morally demanding than socialism. The South Korean experience with baseball and constitutionalism changed the people's traditional moral ecology by teaching them how to be productive individuals. Moral ecologies also possess hidden treasures. Islamic thinkers, for the last seven centuries, have paid very little attention to ideas about human freedom. Apropos other religious frameworks in which moral ecologies (a reservoir of potential spiritual capital) might measure spiritual capital differently, Novak points to the example provided by Aristotle, who taught people how to make a city function without reference to divine revelation. Aristotle provides a precedent and model for talking about spiritual capital without reference to a particular religious creed. This notion confirms Stark's point, however bombastically made, that the lack of religion would have negative economic consequences. One can conclude that a favorable moral ecology is much cheaper than an unfavorable one. It is a thrifty as well as a moral direction.

Recently the Spiritual Enterprise Institute inaugurated an annual *Gallup Poll* on the "Spiritual State of the Union." This in-depth study examines the role of spiritual commitment in many facets of life as well as society as a whole, and it makes it abundantly clear that you can't understand America without an awareness and understanding of its spiritual underpinnings. In fact, the deeper the spiritual commitment of U.S. citizens (their religious and spiritual beliefs and practices), the more profound the impact. If spiritual capital is so critical to moral ecology and individual behavior as well as community action, then what is the spiritual state of the union? Every year the President goes before the combined houses of Congress—the House of Representatives and the Senate—to deliver what has come to be called the state of the union address. It does not address the spiritual state of play, but perhaps it should.

This study was designed to provide a fresh look at how religious and spiritual beliefs relate to current problems, to the economy, and to work; to volunteerism and the giving of money; to meaning and purpose in life; and to people's outlook to the future. Several channels of cultural influence are covered in the survey, including entertainment, business and the workplace, church, politics, and the media.

Scientific survey research plays a vital role in illuminating the fundamental forces that drive humanity. Many social observers maintain the importance of spiritual and moral forces, not just economic and political. Therefore, survey research is poised to make a solid contribution in this century to understanding the spiritual underpinnings of humankind, yielding a great deal more "spiritual information." Polling organizations already survey cross-culturally many different external experiences. The continuing challenge to survey researchers, sociologists, and others is to devise measurements that are useful for understanding people's internal experiences as well. These, after all, are the most important experiences for understanding and improving life. Whether because of noninterest and skepticism about religious or spiritual matters, or the belief that it is pointless to attempt to measure the "immeasurable," it wasn't until the final decades of the last century that social scientists turned their full attention to the inner life. Media commentators, furthermore, routinely ignored this dimension of life in their assessments of the state of the nation.

In the Spiritual Enterprise Institute Poll conducted in 2007,[11] a majority of U.S. adults says that the overall health of the nation, including economic health, depends on the spiritual health of the U.S. A majority also says that success in life is pretty much determined by religious or spiritual forces. A solid majority also says that their religious and spiritual beliefs affect how they invest or save money; their relationships with other people at work; the field of work they have chosen; volunteer activities; entertainment choices, news resources relied upon; and even feelings about the future.

Broadly speaking, spirituality is defined (Webster) as "sensitivity or attachment to religious values and things of the spirit rather than worldly or material interests." When a sample of the public was asked in earlier Gallup surveys what the word "spirituality" meant to them, they gave these responses most frequently: belief in God; a higher power; something beyond oneself; and sense of awe and mystery in the universe; inner peace; state of mind; seeking to be a good person; seeking the inner self; reaching human potential; what has been learned from upbringing, school, church, and the Bible. By a ratio of seven to two, Americans think of spirituality more in a "personal and individual sense" than in terms of "organized religious and church doctrine."

It appears that an increased number of people like the label "spiritual." The percentage of Americans saying they are "spiritual but not religious" has increased ten points since a survey conducted in 1999. In the 2007 survey, only a slightly greater proportion describe themselves as "religious," with 49% saying this, compared to 40% who say they are "spiritual but not religious." Another 7% say they are "both religious and spiritual" and 3% "neither." Coupled with the decline in popularity of the "religious" descriptor has been a six-point drop since a 2002 survey in the percentage of persons saying they are part of the "Christian religious tradition." Those indicating they have "no religious tradition" have grown five percentage points from the earlier surveys in the beginning of the decade.

At the same time, a decline of 14 points is found between the 2002 and 2006 surveys in the percentage that say the overall health of the nation depends greatly on the spiritual health of the nation. In addition, slight declines are recorded in terms of those who say they are active in a church or faith community and in those who say they feel a need to experience spiritual growth in their lives. Whether these declines presage a wholesale decline in religious, and specifically Christian, commitment is much too early to say. Basic beliefs in God and in the divinity of Jesus Christ have remained firm, as have other basic Christian beliefs. Perhaps the most important fact to know about Americans is that they believe, in varying degrees, in a God who is active and vitally interested in humans and who has plans for their lives. Many today are seeking to have a deeper connection with this God or divine power. When the spiritual component is lost, philosophers have long pointed out that societies and economies decline rather than grow. When spirituality abounds, societies, economies, and companies prosper. Clearly, the "State of the Union" depends, in considerable measure, on the *spiritual* state of the union. Such a conclusion is based on both direct and indirect evidence: through self-appraisal, and through an analysis of responses to questions about the level of spiritual commitment in surveys. Regionally, people in the South cared more about ethical/moral issues; in the East, terrorism; the Midwest, Iraq; and the West, education. In the 2007 survey, Republicans cared much more about moral decline; Democrats about poor leadership. Liberals were twice as unhappy about the general economy as Conservatives were.

This survey-based study also focused on "change agents" in U.S. society—the "movers and shakers," the people who "make things happen"—and the role religious and spiritual beliefs play in their lives and their activities. Seven groups of "change agents" were identified: news consumers, innovators, activators, those who want to be heard, eager leaders, "advance" men and women, and public entrepreneurs. The last group represents the net of those saying a "great deal" to the previous groups on the basis of those saying "a great deal" to the question: "To what extent do the following describe you personally—a great deal, somewhat, hardly at all, or not at all?"

It is important to try to shed light on these groups of "change agents" to gain insight into ways to encourage rapid and positive change in society. In an article titled "For God's Eye," Charles Murray of The American Enterprise Institute writes: "A major stream of accomplishment is fostered by a culture in which talented people believe that life has a purpose—that Christianity is a theology 'that empowers and energizes individuals as no other philosophy or religion ever did before'—that it is harder to pursue life's purpose over the years if one is not a believer."[12]

The findings of this 2007 study were examined on the basis of demographics but also by seven groups of "change agents" and by other groupings (based on indices of multiple questions): persons who are highly satisfied with their work; those who say faith brings success; strong activists;

regular contributors of funds; ethical workers and those who believe that the economic health of the nation is related to the spiritual health of the nation. Examination of the survey data by these groups offers further important insights into the role of spirituality in society.

The 13 statement *Spiritual Commitment Index* is the centerpiece of the study and is a trend measurement from an earlier survey. This index includes carefully developed and tested statements about one's faith. This question was asked: "Now, turning to religious and spiritual attitudes, using a scale of zero to five, where 0 means it does not apply at all to you and 5 means it applies completely to you, to what extent do you agree or disagree with the following statements?" The Index included such statements as "My faith is involved in every aspect of my life." "Because of my faith, I have meaning and purpose in my life." "I am a person who is spiritually committed." Based on this scale, one in five (18%) of the adult population in the U.S. can be described as "highly spiritually committed." This 18% represents adults who agreed (4 or 5 on a six-point scale) with each of the 13 statements.

A somber public mood was the backdrop to the 2007 study. Satisfaction with the direction the nation is taking is at a ten-year low. Approval ratings of the executive and legislative branches of government are at a very low point. No fewer than 18 problems are named by a substantial number of Americans as the "most important problem facing the nation today." A wide range of societal problems is tearing at the fabric of American society, with seemingly no clear solutions at hand.

Politically and religiously, the public currently leans to the conservative side of the scale, but relatively few place themselves in the "far right" or "far left." The Iraq war and related issues emerge as the number one issue in the minds of voters today. But when the sample is asked to name other major problems, no fewer than four in ten cite economic problems. Rising fuel prices are noted most often. In times of peace and little threat of war, problems related to the economy invariably rise to the top of the public's list of national concerns.

De Tocqueville, it seems, had it right. Rather than succumb to the multitude of problems that afflict our society, the public, in dramatic fashion, is fighting back. The current study finds that as many as seven in ten adults volunteered for at least one organization in 2007 One third reported that they volunteered for three or more organizations during this time period. The average number of hours volunteered is 4.3 hours per week. Furthermore, seven in ten report regularly contributing money to some group or organization, annually, with frequent churchgoers, college graduates, strong activists, and the highly spiritually committed leading the way. Three in ten persons say they contribute $1,000 or more in a given year. With high levels of people volunteering and contributing money to various causes, "generosity" can certainly be considered to be one of America's greatest traits—and possibly the best hope for the future of the nation.

Much of the volunteerism and giving is spurred by religious and spiritual motivations, often by people's response to what they feel to be God's call on their lives. In this survey, economic health is strongly linked to spiritual health. Sixty-five percent of Americans volunteer a great deal or some versus 81% for churchgoers, 87% for those self-identified as born again, and 89% for spiritually committed. There is such a thing as spiritual capital! Churches and other faith communities play a pivotal role in the volunteerism and giving in this country and are thus one of most cost-effective institutions in society. Without the high level of volunteerism and giving recorded in this survey, the tax burden on the populace would be crushing.

The American people at the present time tend to be bearish about economic conditions, with two thirds saying that economic conditions are "only fair" or "poor." Nevertheless, a majority has genuine confidence in our basic economic system, with 54% seeing it as the "best system we could possibly have" or is "basically okay, but in need of some tinkering." Actually, the percentage that has positive views about the U.S. economic system is higher today than found in a 1992 survey conducted by Gallup. Clearly, spirituality, called "America's greatest energy" by many pundits and comprising religious and spiritual beliefs and practices, has a major role to play in the nation's economy in terms of volunteerism and giving; in seeing one's work as a response to God's plan for one's life; in encouraging open expressions of religion in the workplace; in terms of building trust and restoring ethics in the workplace; and in terms of such personal characteristics as energy, imagination, compassion, optimism, self-sacrifice, focus, and direction. These findings underscore the view of Harvard economist Robert Barro that "religiosity has important consequences for economic performance." Michael Novak has also written: "Initiative, enterprise, responsibility, community skills, traits, realism, practicality, good service, cheerfulness are necessary both to sound enterprises and to durable republics."

The survey offers much evidence that the Protestant work ethic is "alive and well." Six in ten believe success in life is pretty much determined by religious or spiritual forces. Of those who believe in God, huge majorities say God wants them to do something with their lives that will be useful to the world. Furthermore, a majority of adults believe that hard work guarantees success. More than half think being ethical will pay off economically (85% mostly agree). Most see "business" as a key to the nation's economic strength. Our citizens could, in considerable measures, be described as "capitalists, with big hearts."

Sixty-four percent of employees say that, at present, open expressions of religion at their place of work are either encouraged or tolerated. However, this figure grows to 79% when survey respondents (77% among employees) are asked what they would *like to see* be the case. This uptrend suggests that open expressions of religion may become more common in the workplace, particularly when this figure is coupled with the finding that nearly two thirds of employees say they feel the need to experience spiritual growth in their daily lives. One in five (19%) employees report that there are groups at their place of work that meet regularly for prayer or Bible study. While no trend data are available, it is likely that this figure represents an increase over those in earlier decades.

Although Americans are drawn to the lures of materialism, they should not be labeled "materialists," at least on the basis of this study. For example, six in ten believe success in life is pretty much determined by religious or spiritual forces. A similar proportion say that their faith is involved in every aspect of their lives and an even greater proportion, seven in ten, say that because of their faith, they find meaning and purpose in life. Perhaps, as some pundits have argued, we are shifting from a quantitative economy based on profit, data, and the principle of survival of the fittest to a qualitative economy in which the respect for values, ethics, people, and nature is a prerequisite and not just an option.

Likely related in some measure to these findings on "trust" are other survey results indicating that ethics in the workplace can be described as "shaky." For example, a significant proportion (three in ten) of employees are not ready to say they never behave unethically in their work. In addition, as many as half of employees indicate that they do not feel fully responsible to make sure other employees behave ethically. Only four in ten Americans believe today that, in general, people can be trusted. Six in ten think, "You can't be too careful."

Although this distrust appears to be pervasive, it is somewhat more pronounced among poorer, less educated persons. Those most likely to trust others are college graduates as well as activists and charitable givers. This analysis suggests that trust levels are likely to rise if growing numbers of persons enter the ranks of volunteers and charitable givers.

The findings of this study go far toward the goal of demonstrating the relevance and potential of the notion that spiritual mores demonstrably affect the nation's economy. The spiritual health of the nation is important to 63% of all respondents, 79% of churchgoers, 72 % of Christians, 84% of those born again, but just 44% of liberals.

The results of this study and others like it clearly point to spirituality (religious and spiritual beliefs and practice) as being the fountain out of which flows social capital and human capital. Social capital and human capital themselves are likely based to a large extent on the existence of good faith, trust, stewardship, sense of purpose, and other moral characteristics that cannot persist in the absence of the piety, solidarity, and hope that come from religion and spiritual sentiments. With spiritual forces connected to economic forces in many direct and indirect ways, it behooves those engaged in the field of spiritual enterprise to examine the specifics of this economic-spiritual connection.

Like all forms of capital, spiritual capital formation depends on delayed gratification. Future benefit is weighed against immediate consumption. In the same way that money capital can accumulate in savings accounts and investments, so too can spiritual capital be built up over time through the habits of the heart and realized in mediating structures, such as families, churches and other religious institutions, social groups, schools, and the wider culture. It should be remembered that when critics complain about the lack, or the unequal distribution, of capital in the modern world they too often forget that spiritual capital can be as important as other forms of capital in restoring communities or building nations. This notion of modernization has become more apparent as the previously popular theories about secularization coming with modernization have fallen by the wayside or been contradicted by the stubborn reality of a religious, and probably increasingly religious, world.

The thinkers of the Scottish Enlightenment described what they believed was an innate moral sense, tied at the same time to benevolence, self-love, and the right to contract with others. Adam Smith maintained that the desire to engage in a mutually beneficial voluntary exchange of private property is an innate human propensity. In this view, freedom and responsibility are intrinsic to capital formation: a sense of purpose, moral purpose, can give rise to the formation of every kind of capital, but such purpose can flourish only when it is given freedom, religious freedom, to do so. Modern commerce grew out of this rich religious tradition and is sustained by it in the spirit of democratic capitalism.

The claim that economic freedom and the growth of spiritual capital go together with religious freedom has strong empirical foundations. As we observe in data collected by the likes of Freedom House and others, those states that fail to allow economic freedom are those that do not permit religious liberty either. Likewise, those that fail to encourage religious liberty tend to fail to give rise to free economies.

Dysfunctional societies are desperate places that still exhibit tribalism and internecine warfare, or have come to live like welfare queens—off the fat of the state, which in this case turns out to be the aid system of guilt-ridden developed countries, which are quick to give aid but slow to build or invest in real needs. These regimes remain mired in the past, with no way to break free unless they step out into the risky zone of freedom. If they start with religious liberty they will also get a degree of economic freedom. And if they commence changes in their economic freedoms, they will soon give rise to religious demands for liberty. The mistake is trying to separate forces that are naturally joined.

The creation and renewal of spiritual capital that uniquely generates and sustains real enterprises and other institutions, profit and not-for-profit, require the give and take of discourse and practice across different religious groups, including those that adopt a "non-religious" commitment. Without the opportunity not to believe, there is no real freedom of conscience or religion. So the view presented here allocates a real value to the secular option, but not a monopolizing value. Linking religious liberty and economic freedom to form enterprises of lasting value is the clarion call of humane people, robust economies, and enlightened nations today.

There is an old Puritan hymn we grew up singing; perhaps you recall it:

> *Dare to be a Daniel,*
>
> *Dare to stand alone;*
>
> *Dare to have a purpose firm,*
>
> *Dare to make it known.*

In a famous essay written just after World War II, George Orwell, in one of his great punch lines, suggested, "To bring this hymn up to date one would have to add a 'Don't' at the beginning of each line."[13] He was talking about the timidity of modern people, thinkers and doers alike, in relatively safe circumstances, to be quiet about dishonesty. Doesn't intelligence require truth-telling? But then in the first sentence of *1984* Orwell himself wrote satirically: "It was a bright cold day in April, and the clocks were striking thirteen."

Isn't it time to pull ourselves from the swamp of political correctness and the lies of advertising and a near-total bureaucracy that have consumed so many secular, especially academic, pundits? Global poverty, we are told, is the greatest challenge of our time. Many believe investments in education to be an essential part of the solution to this *grand* challenge. Despite spending $2.3 trillion on development assistance over the past 50 years, as William Easterly reminds us in *White Man's Burden: Why the West's Efforts to Aid the Rest Have Done So Much Ill and So Little Good*, failure abounds.[14] States Easterly: "In foreign aid, Planners announce good intentions but don't motivate anyone to carry them out; Searchers find things that work and get some reward....Planners apply global blueprints; Searchers adapt to local conditions. Planners at the top lack knowledge of the bottom, while Searchers find out what the reality is at the bottom. Planners never hear whether the planned got what it needed; Searchers find out whether the customer is satisfied."

So we ask as searchers, Might it be time for leaders, for philanthropists, for business executives, for politicians, and for the citizenry at large to lead where others fear to tread?

To rethink ways forward, not in some new Plan or millennial goals but merely by utilizing the magic of the market and the well-known reward of thrifty entrepreneurship?

If we ask those questions in the light of the considerations raised in this book, then we are surely guided to thrift, as a much-needed virtue and as an illustration of the true meaning of spiritual capital. I have tried to show the place of thrift in a theological worldview as well as its effects in generating an economy of stewardship rather than consumption. Thrift serves as a link between the spiritual investment and the material reward. And the reward is not merely an increase in productivity but a care for others, for the environment, and for future generations. The economy of thrift is one that bears the imprint of the spiritual legacy from which it springs. It is one that answers both to the demands of environmentalists, that we conserve the earth's resources, and to the demands of philanthropists, that we care for the poor. It is an economy that shows the effect of reinvesting spiritual capital, namely to conserve the permanent resources.

In place of that economy, however, we have seen emerging the economy of transient and consumable things. In this book I have sided with those critics of the consumer society who have seen the fragmentation of the family, the loss of commitment, and the growth of short-term pleasure-seeking as its most evident effects. I agree with them that, even if, in some attenuated economic theory, the consumer society is capable of self-perpetuation in a continual orgy of stale delights, it will provide only an impoverished life to its members. It will be a life without happiness, because without solid virtues, a life in which the old ideas of duty, sacrifice, and responsibility have no place love is dethroned from its place in the center of things.

The remedy for this state of affairs is not more state action, more welfare programs, another bailout, and more interference and regulation from above in the workings of the market. The remedy comes from below, in the reinvestment of spiritual capital. It comes from people once again taking charge of their own lives, seeking to live as those Calvinist Scots of the seventeenth century lived, in a state of responsible stewardship over all resources within their control, saving for the future, spending on others in need, and living a life of good will and piety, according to the law of God.

Perhaps together and by leveraging our minds and resources we can achieve a new revolution in ethical thinking and doing. That's *if* we, as the prophets of Old suggested, dare to be Daniels. Thrift and its sister virtues, if truly embraced and followed, if fueled and lived, if tied to all the other moral virtues, would without doubt lead to greater human flourishing. In fact, as the American framers intended, Benjamin Franklin especially, those virtues would supply us with unprecedented benevolence. The disposition to do well would emanate from an inclination to be charitable and would in the end be a gift from generosity. All of this would occur if the virtue of thrift became less forgotten and, instead, found new favor and life among us all. Its renewal would perhaps be activated if we, like the poet Gerard Manley Hopkins, came to appreciate again the "dappled things":

Glory be to God for dappled things—
For skies of couple-color as a brinded cow;
For rose-moles all in stipple upon trout that swim;
Fresh-firecoal chestnut-falls; finches' wings. . .

All things counter, original, spare, strange;
Whatever is fickle, freckled (who knows how?)
With swift, slow; sweet, sour; adazzle, dim;
He fathers-forth whose beauty is past change:
Praise him.

—*Pied Beauty*
Gerard Manley Hopkins

# ACKNOWLEDGMENTS

> *"A bargain ain't a bargain unless*
> *it's something you need."*
> — Sidney Carroll

All of us have dreams—day dreams, night dreams, and visions, myths that motivate and serve to extol the higher good or memories that appear as shadows to color the traces of our minds and affect our nearly every doing. I admit that I am not a deep sleep or REM expert and certainly have not been trained in psychiatry. Nor am I a *seer*. I have never been occupied, as Joseph in the Old Testament, as an interpreter of dreams.

Some of us have a particular dream that haunts us or comes back like a monster under the bed or a dragon nipping at our toes, even when we think it has been exorcised. I have to acknowledge I don't remember many of my own dreams at all. I sleep soundly and rarely awake startled or shaken, although I am told that I snore. However, I have two dreams that have stayed with me from my youth, so they must mean something, and at least have some definitive bearing on who I am or have become. One is good and the other bad.

The first relates to something my dear mother used to say to me as a very small boy. If ever I was disturbed or unstill at evening's rest, she would say, on tucking me into bed or when I awoke in a midnight fright, "Just remember Lake Pleasant." That, you see, was the near-perfect spot where our family vacationed every summer in the Adirondacks. The aptly named lake was as calm and beautiful as any place in the world, I knew. Just thinking of it put my mind and soul at rest and assured me that all was right with God in His heaven and with His creatures on this earth. It dissipated all my fears and let me focus on what is good, what is true, and what is beautiful. It also made for a restful night's sleep. It was a dream or image that always and still does make everything *all right*. I have to admit that even in the very learned circles I travel in today I still picture Lake Pleasant whenever I need to find inner peace and be centered. It is, I suppose, what T.S. Eliot called the *still point*.

> *At the still point of the turning world. Neither flesh nor fleshless;*
>
> *Neither from nor towards; at the still point, there the dance is,*
>
> *But neither arrest nor movement. And do not call it fixity,*
>
> *Where past and future are gathered. Neither movement from nor towards,*
>
> *Neither ascent nor decline. Except for the point, the still point,*
>
> *There would be no dance, and there is only the dance.*
>
> **"Burnt Norton," Four Quartets**

The other dream was (perhaps is, because I still have it) alarming. I grew up in the center of the hustle and bustle of the city of Brotherly Love, Philadelphia, in the 1950s and

60s. We were an affluent, upper-middle-class, Protestant (Presbyterian) family, with a Scottish surname and Old Dutch family roots. Whatever I wanted, I more or less got. In the post-World War II boom, the economy went just one direction, *up*. We had two cars in the garage, a good roof over our head, a stable home life and extended family surrounding, embracing, and protecting us. We never went hungry—far from it. Very different from my parents' Depression generation, we wanted for absolutely nothing. Our motto was "ask and it shall be given." There was a Santa Claus, and he brought many gifts, not only in late December. Church on Sunday confirmed our faith, the place where we sang the *doxology*, praising God from whom every blessing flowed. But my parents were not liberal, do-nothing, free-ride types. Hardly... They came from the school of hard knocks: You get what you work for, and what you deserve. They lived and preached the old-fashioned Protestant work ethic. My grandparents came from Scottish stock that fled the poverty of the old world to gain economic independence and find riches in the new one. They never shirked effort or toil. Quite the opposite, they typically sought it out; for them, work saved you in this world, and the next.

They and their ilk believed that you were rewarded as a measure of the risk, sacrifice, and dedication you personally took on yourself. I can still see and hear my Scottish grandfather, with his oversized, wiry eyebrows and distinctive brogue, reminding us that the playing of cards was an admission of "idle time." Needless to say, there was little drink and no gambling in his orbit. He worked 60-hour weeks, speculated in land even through the Depression, and lived to the ripe old age of 102, working to the very end. He was also tight with the coin—what he called *Thrifty!* So much so that I can recall family stories about him walking four miles to save a quarter bus fare, even though he was not a poor man. On our country farm in Lancaster County my grandparents grew fruits and vegetables, reared sheep and geese, but most memorably for me they used the Yellow Pages as toilet paper. Always saving!

It should come as no surprise then that as early as possible I too was asked or, rather, expected to work, to do assigned chores, and to earn what they called an allowance. I was paid to *do* things, such as collect and recycle old newspapers and metal cans, take out the trash, polish shoes, or cut the lawn. We could have afforded to have others or hired hands do these things, but why was that necessary when my parents had two boys who needed to learn the "value of things"? I distinctly recall having a PSFS savings book account in grade school and making deposits in it every week (the cover was also Scotch plaid), so that when Christmas came around I would have saved enough to buy everyone a decent gift. My parents instituted a regime where I got paid for every "A" on my report card. Scholarship was regarded highly, and education was viewed as the pathway ahead and to betterment. It's not surprising, therefore, that I got almost all As for years and years, right into high school and throughout college. But back to this recurring dream, the ominous one.

At about age eleven, or fifth grade, I applied for and was accepted without much parental prodding to become a paperboy for the afternoon news daily, *The Philadelphia*

*Bulletin.* I was, I think, the youngest boy in the branch but was fortunate to get one of the very best routes. I had about a hundred houses in a three-street area that included my own block. Every afternoon after school I would race home and get on my bicycle, with a large basket attached to the handlebars, then speed back to the storage garage where all the papers were dropped off, so as to gather and fold mine for *very* rapid delivery. The faster I got finished the sooner I could go on to play basketball, baseball, or football, which were my real youthful avocations. I could after a while do the entire route in less than thirty minutes, throwing papers and being quite expert in every facet of delivery. I was so good, in fact, that I both made lots of money (relative to an average 11- or 12-year-old) and got huge tips from my highly pleased customers. I was forced to save at least half of what I earned. I had blond hair and blue eyes and said "please" and "thank you" a lot, and people seemed to reward those traits as well. I also sold accident insurance that the paper company offered. I so excelled as a salesman that I won an all-expense trip to EXPO '67 in Montreal for selling more new nickel policies than anybody else in the city. I was a good, well, if I must say so, outstanding, paperboy.

The one problem with this scenario was the dream I had every fortnight or so. It was a dream about forgetting to pick up and deliver my papers and the ruckus it caused to all those who depended on me for this service and their news. I would often wake up in the middle of the night worried and shaken deeply that I had been so irresponsible. But, of course, I had done nothing of the sort. It was *only a bad dream.* I never missed a single day, or I arranged for substitutes. But to this day that dream or at least the memory of it haunts me. Does that kind of virtuous duty, of thrift rewarded by hard work, of responsibility, remain an American, a global value? In an age of entitlement and overly pampered children, where affluence leads to decadence, does any community any longer bother to instill the meaning and esteem for work as an *ethic*, in word and deed? Has thrift truly become a lost or forgotten virtue? Can it ever be rediscovered, restored?

One of the lasting memories I have of my childhood involved another ritual. It wasn't going to the YMCA, although we did that, or reading the scripture in church, although I did that, or going to a mission on Delaware Avenue to dispense a cup of soup, although we did that, or having to take trumpet lessons every week at Zapf's on Fifth Street, although I did that (and my brother took tenor saxophone). This other formative and regular occurrence was my father taking, at times dragging, his young sons to the Philadelphia Public Library every other week, usually on Friday night or Saturday morning. Once there we each had to choose three or four books that we had to finish reading by the time we returned. This forced reading program no doubt improved my vocabulary considerably and likely helped to turn me into an intellectual at an early stage, but it also shaped me into a voracious reader and seeker of knowledge. I loved social studies and politics, but my favorite *genre* was biography. I must have consumed hundreds of biographies in my youth about presidents, captains of industry, famous generals, religious leaders (Catholic, Protestant, and Jewish), adventurers, and sports stars. I still remember books about

Thomas Jefferson, Benjamin Franklin, John Kennedy, Babe Ruth, Lewis & Clark, Andrew Carnegie, and naturally Theodore Roosevelt. I believe there is nothing like the stories of biography and autobiography to motivate a young person. They both hold out an ideal and demonstrate the practice of accomplishment—*the thrill of victory and the agony of defeat*, to quote an old sports tagline. We need to read more biographies, young and old alike, to (re)discover *heroes*: practitioners of virtues, and especially of thrift.

No book—biography or scientific analysis, and especially this one—is ever totally one's own work, since we have been shaped and influenced by so many people, teachers, ideas, movements, and other books. I do take responsibility for what is here said, omitted, or argued, poorly or well. In humility, I think I know only some small part of what is knowable on this or any given subject. But I have always been willing to perpetually learn. I appreciate the life of example given to me by my grandparents and parents and by my sole sibling, my younger brother, Richard, who has prospered well and become a corporate leader. My children have surely affected me in ways I can hardly even comprehend. They remain my dearest and best friends, in whom I take true pride and great joy. I love my wife, Beth, who endures me.

I am particularly grateful for meeting and being challenged by a real hero, Sir John Templeton, the famous investor and legendary philanthropist. I readily admit that funding for research leading to this book was made possible through the generosity of his foundation. His own life is indeed a testimony to the virtue of thrift. I was moved and delighted that he consented to write the *Foreword* to this book for me before he passed away, and it may be the last thing he wrote as old age crept in on his abundant, productive, and most generous life.

I am also grateful to the Spiritual Enterprise Institute, which I founded and whose board I chair, for prodding me to write such a book and collect my jumble of ideas. Some of the original thoughts were shaped by a symposium roundtable on "the two moralities" convened at a lovely spa at Tunbridge Wells, in Kent, England, by the Social Affairs Unit. This is a think tank in the United Kingdom that has built up a deserved reputation for recovering the wisdom of the ages and critiquing the decadence of the phony values that have overtaken in many cases the lasting virtues handed down from classical antiquity, from the Hebrew Bible and from a hitherto unbroken tradition of Judeo-Christian moral teaching.

**Theodore Roosevelt Malloch**
Jupiter Island, Florida
2009

# ENDNOTES

### INTRODUCTION

[1] *Webster's Dictionary*, 1ˢᵗ ed. (1828).

[2] Gertrude Himmelfarb, "From Victorian Virtues to Modern Values," (paper presented at the AEI Bradley Lecture Series, February 13, 1995), p.1. The longer book treatment is *The De-Moralization of Society: From Victorian Virtues to Modern Values*.

### CHAPTER 1

[1] John Calvin, *Institutes of the Christian Religion*, 1559 translation ed. (Westminster: John Knox Press, 1960).

[2] John Calvin, *Commentaries* (Grand Rapids: Baker Books, 1974).

[3] John Calvin, *Commentary on Matthew*, 6.31-43.

[4] ibid.

[5] ibid.

[6] ibid.

[7] ibid.

[8] ibid.

[9] ibid. Christopher Dawson, the social historian, speaks highly of Augustine's social ethic in *Progress and Religion* (Washington, DC: Catholic University Press, 2001) when he says, "In the West, under the influence of Augustine, Christianity became a dynamic moral and social force" (p. 67).

[10] Deirdre N. McCloskey, *Bourgeois Virtues: Ethics for an Age of Commerce* (Chicago: University of Chicago Press, 2007).

[11] Max Weber, *The Protestant Ethic and the Spirit of Capitalism* (New York: Penguin, 1965). Simon Schama provides a historiographical critique of the connection drawn between specific tenets of Calvinist theology and a study of spending habits in Dutch society in his tome, *The Embarrassment of Riches: An Interpretation of Dutch Culture in the Golden Age* (New York: Vintage, 1997). Paul Marshall's thesis in *A Kind of Life Imposed on Man: Vocation and Social Order from Tyndale to Locke* (Toronto: University of Toronto Press, 1996) provides an alternate and different interpretation on Weber and Locke.

[12] Calvin, *Commentary*.

### CHAPTER 2

[1] Christopher Lasch, *The True and Only Heaven: Progress and Its Critics* (New York: W.W. Norton, 1991).

[2] John De Graff, David Wann, and Thomas H. Naylor, *Affluenza: The All-Consuming Epidemic* (San Francisco: Berrett-Koehler Publishers, 2003).

[3] Theodore Schultz, *Economic Crisis in World Agriculture* (Ann Arbor: University of Michigan Press, 1965).

[4] World Bank report.

[5] W.W. Rostow, *The Process of Economic Growth* (New York: W.W. Norton, 1962).

[6] P.T. Bauer, *Dissent on Development* (Cambridge: Harvard University Press, 1992).

[7] Fernando Henrique Cardoso and Faletto Enzo, *Dependency and Development in Latin America* (Berkeley: University of California Press, 1979).

[8] Robert M. Solow, *Growth Theory* (New York, Oxford University Press, 2000).

[9] Nigel Healey, *Development Economics* (London: Heinemann, 1984).

[10] W. M. Flinn, *Survey of Agricultural Economics* (Ann Arbor: University of Michigan Press, 1964).

[11] R. Havens, *Development Economics*, 5th ed. (New York: W.W. Norton, 2002).

[12] Paul Rodan, *Latin American Theory and Development* (New York: Harper, 1974).

[13] Amartya Sen, *Development as Freedom* (New York: Anchor, 2000).

[14] R.F. Harrod, *International Trade Theory* (New York: MacMillan, 1963).

[15] Peter Berger, *Pyramids of Sacrifice* (New York: Anchor, 2000) p.13.

[16] Sir Brian Heap, *Towards Sustainable Consumption* (London: The Royal Society, 2000).

[17] David Myers, *The Pursuit of Happiness* (New York: Harper, 1993).

[18] *Condorcet: Selected Writings* (New York: MacMillan Publishing, 1976) p. 221.

[19] Kenneth J. Arrow, *Social Choice and Individual Values* (New Haven: Yale University Press, 1970).

## CHAPTER 3

[1] Aristotle, *The Nicomachean Ethic* (Oxford: Oxford University Press, 1998).

[2] John Templeton, Jr., MD, *Thrift and Generosity: The Joy of Giving* (Philadelphia: The Templeton Foundation Press, 2004).

[3] ibid., p. 41.

[4] ibid., p. 42.

[5] ibid., p. 6.

[6] George Steiner, *Lessons of the Masters* (Cambridge: Harvard University Press, 2005).

[7] Alistair MacIntyre, *After Virtue* (South Bend: Notre Dame University Press, 2007).

[8] G.E.M. Anscombe "Modern Moral Philosophy" in Bernard Williams' "Moral Dilemmas" (Cambridge: Cambridge University Press, 2004).

[9] Stephen G. Post, *Why Good Things Happen to Good People* (New York: Broadway, 2008).

[10] Christopher Peterson and Martin E. P. Seligman, eds. *Character Strengths and Virtues: A Handbook and Classification* (New York: Oxford University Press, 2004).

## CHAPTER 4

[1] James Collier, *The Rise of Selfishness in America* (New York: American Philological Association, 1991).

[2] ibid.

[3] ibid.

[4] ibid.

5 Robert J. Samuelson, "America's Low Savings Rate Not as Bad as it Sounds," *The Register Guard*. Aug. 17, 2005. http://news.google.com/newspapers?nid=1310&dat=20050817&id=Kn8VAAAAIBAJ&sjid=efADAAAAIBAJ&pg=2888,3629573

**CHAPTER 5**

1 Martin Buber, *Good and Evil* (New York: Macmillan, 1980), p. 45.

2 Hans Kohn, *Nationalism: The New Realities and the Old Myths* (New York: Harcourt Brace Jovanovich, 1972).

3 ibid., p. 51.

4 Eric Fromm, *The Sane Society* (New York: Fawcett, 1977), p. 29.

5 Carl von Clausewitz, *On War* (Harmondsworth: Penguin, 1968), p. 119.

6 David Ziegler, *War, Peace and International Politics* (Boston: Little Brown, 1997), pp. 75-93.

7 Martin Rein, *Scial Science and Public Policy* (New York: Penguin, 1976).

8 Joan Robinson, *What are the Questions and Other Essays* (London: M.E. Sharpe, 1981), p. 24.

9 Barbara Ward, *Five Ideas that Changed the World* (New York: Norton, 1959) p. 42.

10 Harry Blaimers, *The Christian Mind* (London: Crossway, 1970), p. 23.

11 George F. Kennan, *American Diplomacy* (Chicago: Chicago University Press, 1985) p. 146. See also his *Nuclear Delusion* (New York: Pantheon Books, 1982), and *Soviet Foreign Policy* (Westwood: Greenwood Press, 1978), where his views are revised.

12 Zbigniew Brzezinski, *In Quest of National Security Policy* (New York: Farrar, Straus and Giroux, 1988), p. 101.

13 C.S. Lewis, *The Four Loves* (London: Geoffrey Bles, 1960), p. 38.

14 As quoted by Lewis in *The Four Loves*, p. 33.

15 A.J.P. Taylor, *A Personal History* (London: Athenaeum, 1983), p. 95.

**CHAPTER 6**

1 Thomas Stewart, "12 Management Tips for Slow Times," *Business 2.0*, February 1, 2002, p.1.

2 ibid.

3 ibid., p. 2.

4 Savings banks are described at length in ASB Bank Ltd. bank report, 2001.

5 Adam Smith, *The Wealth of Nations* (New York: Prometheus Books, 2003).

6 John Meynard Keynes, *The General Theory of Employment, Interest and Money* (New York: Prometheus Books, 2002).

7 George Weigel, *The Cube and the Cathedral* (New York: Basic Books, 2005), p. 14.

8 Richard Weaver, *Ideas Have Consequences* (Chicago: University of Chicago Press, 1984), p. 131.

**CHAPTER 7**

1 Robert Lane, *Political Ideology* (New York: Free Press, 1962).

2 Kenneth Minogue, *The Liberal Mind* (Indianapolis: Liberty Fund, 2001).

[3] Steve Jobs, 2005 Standford University commencement address, June 12, 2005. http://news.stanford.edu/news/2005/june15/jobs-061505.html

[4] Max Dupree, *Leadership Jazz* (New York: Dell, 1993), p. 23.

[5] N.T. Wright, *Simply Christian* (San Francisco: Harper, 2006), p. 54.

[6] Josef Pieper, *Lesiure, the Basis of Culture* (Indianapolis: Liberty Fund, 1999), p.86.

**CHAPTER 8**

[1] *The Best of Edmund Burke: Selected Writings and Speeches* (Washington, D.C.: Regnery Publishing, 2000).

[2] Himmelfarb, "From Victorian Virtues to Modern Values," p. 15.

[3] Lytton Strachey, *Eminent Victorians* (Oxford: Oxford University Press, 2009). This is a critique of the well-known work by A.N. Wilson, *The Victorians* (New York: W.W. Norton, 2003), which pictured eminent Victorians as stupid and prudish.

[4] Walter Lippmann, *The Decline of Western Democracy* (New York: Transaction, 1999), p. 39.

[5] ibid., p. 27.

[6] ibid., p. 33.

[7] Michael Lindsay, *Faith in the Halls of Power* (New York: Oxford University Press, 2007).

[8] Rodney Stark, *Victory of Reason* (New York: Random House, 2006).

[9] Robert Barro, *Determinants of Economic Growth* (Cambridge: MIT Press, 1998).

[10] Michael Novak, *The Universal Hunger for Liberty* (New York: Basic Books, 2006).

[11] This and all of the following surveys mentioned are proprietary surveys by the Spiritual Enterprise Institute conducted by The Gallup Organization and are not publicly available.

[12] Charles Murray, *Human Accomplishment* (New York: Harper Perennial, 2004), p 128.

[13] George Orwell, *Collection of Essays* (New York: Mariner, 1970), p. 39.

[14] William Easterly, *White Man's Burden: Why the West's Efforts to Aid the Rest Have Done So Much Ill and So Little Good* (New York: Penguin, 2007), p. 331.

# Heroes of Thrift

Are there any heroes of thrift from whom we moderns and now post-moderns or post-post-moderns can learn? I think there are at least three such persons, and perhaps many more, who exhibit distinctive models of thrift and from whose examples we can benefit.

## BENJAMIN FRANKLIN

Colonial America provides me with my first stalwart of thrift: the revolutionary statesman, inventor, and publisher, Benjamin Franklin. This widely admired figure possessed an endearing wit and charm. His practical intelligence and commitment to virtues, especially thrift, were well known. He viewed industry as admirable. Franklin's contribution to modern political thought should not be underestimated. The range of his ideas spans letters, essays, pamphlets, political documents, and an annual Almanac. His quippish sayings are renowned and of lasting value even in our present age. Some of the most pertinent to thrift are:

> He that builds before he counts the cost acts foolishly; and he that counts before he builds, finds he did not count wisely.
>
> Patience in market is worth pounds in a year.

An egg today is better than a hen tomorrow.

All things are cheap to the saving, dear to the wasteful.

Would you live with ease? Do what you ought, not what you please.

As America's leading diplomat during the American Revolution, Franklin secured alliance with the French, which helped to make independence possible. He was greatly noted for his curiosity. His diverse writings, some expressly political and others highly scientific, gained him a robust popularity. As a leader of the Enlightenment, he won recognition from scientists and intellectuals across Europe. An agent in London before the Revolution and minister to France during the war, he more than anyone else defined the new nation in the minds of Europe. His success in securing French military and financial aid was a great contribution to the American victory over Britain. He invented the lightning rod, bifocals, the iron furnace stove (also known as the Franklin stove), a carriage odometer, and a musical instrument known as the armonica. He was an early proponent of colonial unity. Many historians hail him as the "First American" or the "quintessential American."

Born in colonial Boston, Massachusetts, of strict Calvinist parentage, Franklin learned printing from his older brother and became a newspaper editor, printer, and merchant in Philadelphia, gaining considerable wealth. He spent many years in England and published the famous

*Poor Richard's Almanac* and the *Pennsylvania Gazette*. He formed both the first public lending library and fire department in America as well as the Junto, a political discussion club. During his younger years he wrote in favor of paper money and against mercantilist policies such as the Iron Act of 1750; he also drafted, in 1754, the Albany Plan of Union, which would have created a continental legislature, demonstrating how early he conceived of the colonies as being naturally one political unit.

Franklin became a national hero in America when he spearheaded the effort to have Parliament repeal the unpopular Stamp Act. An accomplished diplomat, he was widely admired among the French as American minister to Paris and was a major figure in the development of positive Franco-American relations. From 1775 to 1776, Franklin was Postmaster General under the Continental Congress and from 1785 to 1788 was President of the Supreme Executive Council of Pennsylvania. Toward the end of his life, he became one of the most prominent abolitionists.

Franklin was interested in science and technology, carrying out his famous electricity experiments and inventing many items. He also played a major role in establishing the University of Pennsylvania and Franklin and Marshall College. In 1769, he was elected the first president of the American Philosophical Society, the oldest learned society in the United States. Franklin was fluent in five languages.

Like the other advocates of republicanism, Franklin emphasized that the new republic could survive only if the people were virtuous in the sense of attention to civic duty and rejection of corruption. Indeed, all his life he explored the role of civic and personal virtue, as expressed in *Poor Richard's* aphorisms.

Although Franklin's parents had intended for him to have a career in the church, Franklin became disillusioned with organized religion after discovering deism. *"I soon became a thorough Deist."* He went on to attack Christian principles of free will and morality in a 1725 pamphlet, *A Dissertation on Liberty and Necessity, Pleasure and Pain.* He consistently attacked religious dogma, arguing that morality was more dependent on virtue and benevolent actions than on strict obedience to religious orthodoxy: *"I think opinions should be judged by their influences and effects; and if a man holds none that tend to make him less virtuous or more vicious, it may be concluded that he holds none that are dangerous, which I hope is the case with me."* A few years later, Franklin repudiated his 1725 pamphlet as an embarrassing "erratum." In 1790, just about a month before he died, Franklin wrote the following in a letter to Ezra Stiles, president of Yale, who had asked him his views on religion:

> "As to Jesus of Nazareth, my opinion of whom you particulary desire, I think the System of Morals and his Religion, as he left them to us, the best the world ever saw or is likely to see; but I apprehend it has received various corrupt changes, and I have, with most of the present Dissenters in England, some Doubts as to his divinity; though it is a question I do not dogmatize upon, having never studied it and I think it

needless to busy myself with it now, when I expect soon an Opportunity of knowing the Truth
with less Trouble..."

Like most Enlightenment intellectuals, Franklin separated virtue, morality, and faith from organized religion,
although he felt that if religion in general grew weaker,
morality, virtue, and society in general would also decline.
Thus he wrote Thomas Paine: *"If men are so wicked with religion, what would they be if without it."* According to academic
experts, Franklin was a proponent of all religions. He prayed
to *"Powerful Goodness"* and referred to God as the *"INFINITE."*
John Adams noted that Franklin was a mirror in which people saw their own religion: "The Catholics thought him almost a Catholic. The Church of England claimed him as one
of them. The Presbyterians thought him half a Presbyterian,
and the Friends believed him a wet Quaker." Whatever else
Benjamin Franklin was, concludes Adams, "he was a true
champion of generic religion." Ben Franklin was noted to
be "the spirit of the Enlightenment."

In his excellent recent biography, Walter Isaacson argues that Franklin became uncomfortable with an unen-
hanced version of deism and came up with his own conception of the Creator. Franklin outlined his concept of
deity in 1728, in his "Articles of Belief and Acts of Religion."
From this document, Isaacson compares Franklin's conception of deity to that of strict deists and orthodox Christians.
Isaacson concludes that, unlike most pure deists, Franklin
believed that a faith in God should inform our daily actions,
but that, like other deists, his faith was devoid of sectarian

dogma. Isaacson also discusses Franklin's conception that God had created beings who do interfere in wordly matters, which for some is evidence of Franklin embracing some sort of polytheism, with a bevy of lesser gods overseeing various realms and planets.

On July 4, 1776, Congress appointed a committee that included Benjamin Franklin, Thomas Jefferson, and John Adams to design the Great Seal of the United States. This committee created and approved the first proposed design for the seal (which ultimately was not adopted). Each member of the committee proposed a unique design: Franklin's proposal featured a design with the motto: "Rebellion to Tyrants is Obedience to God." This design was to portray a scene from the Book of Exodus, complete with Moses, the Israelites, the pillar of fire, and George III depicted as Pharaoh.

At the Constitutional Convention in 1787, when the convention seemed headed for disaster due to heated debate, the elderly Franklin displayed his conviction of a deity intimately involved in human affairs by requesting that each day's session begin with prayers. Franklin recalled the days of the Revolutionary War, when the American leaders assembled in prayer daily, seeking "divine guidance" from the "Father of lights." He then rhetorically asked, *"And have we now forgotten that powerful friend? Or do we imagine that we no longer need his assistance?"*

Although Franklin may have financially supported one particular Presbyterian group in Philadelphia, apparently he never formally joined any particular Christian denomination or any other religion. According to the epitaph Franklin wrote for himself at an early age, it is clear that he believed in a physical resurrection of the body some time after death. Whether this belief was held throughout his life is unclear.

Franklin sought to cultivate his character by a plan of thirteen *virtues*, which he developed at age 20 (in 1726) and continued to practice in some form for the rest of his life. His autobiography lists his thirteen virtues as:

1. "TEMPERANCE. Eat not to dullness; drink not to elevation."

2. "SILENCE. Speak not but what may benefit others or yourself; avoid trifling conversation."

3. "ORDER. Let all your things have their places; let each part of your business have its time."

4. "RESOLUTION. Resolve to perform what you ought; perform without fail what you resolve."

5. "FRUGALITY. Make no expense but to do good to others or yourself; i.e., waste nothing."

6. "INDUSTRY. Lose no time; be always employ'd in something useful; cut off all unnecessary actions."

7. "SINCERITY. Use no hurtful deceit; think innocently and justly, and, if you speak, speak accordingly."

8. "JUSTICE. Wrong none by doing injuries, or omitting the benefits that are your duty."

9. "MODERATION. Avoid extremes; forbear re-
   senting injuries so much as you think they
   deserve."

10. "CLEANLINESS. Tolerate no uncleanliness in
    body, cloaths, or habitation."

11. "TRANQUILLITY. Be not disturbed at trifles,
    or at accidents common or unavoidable."

12. "CHASTITY. Rarely use venery but for health
    or offspring, never to dullness, weakness, or
    the injury of your own or another's peace or
    reputation."

13. "HUMILITY. Imitate Jesus and Socrates."

## SAMUEL SMILES

In the 1870s the world deemed a gifted Scotsman, Samuel
Smiles, author of the best-selling book *Self-Help*, an international celebrity. Translated into many languages and
inscribed on walls around the world, his words held great
sway for decades but are now largely forgotten. At his death
the funeral cortege was nearly as long as Queen Victoria's.

The wisdom of Smiles is absorbing. The strength lies
in its ethical dimension. He called this "character." It meant
much more than mere obedience to regulations or business
ethics. His other books, *Character* (1871), *Thrift* (1875), and
*Duty* (1880), give a flavor of a remorseless advocacy of virtue. Together they are a library of wisdom about the virtue
of thrift in building character and bonding individuals in
noble pursuits.

Samuel Smiles, the eldest of 11 children, was born on
December 23, 1812. Samuel's parents ran a small general store

in Haddington, Scotland. After attending the local school, he left at 14 and joined Dr. Robert Lewins as an apprentice. After making good progress with Dr. Lewins, Smiles went to Edinburgh University in 1829 to study medicine. While in Edinburgh, Smiles became involved in the campaign for parliamentary reform. During this period he had several articles on the subject published by the progressive *Edinburgh Weekly Chronicle*.

Smiles graduated in 1832 and found work as a doctor in Haddington. He continued to take a close interest in politics and became a strong supporter of Joseph Hume, the Scottish radical politician from Montrose. Hume, like Smiles, had trained as a doctor.

In 1837 Samuel Smiles began contributing articles on parliamentary reform for the *Leeds Times*. The following year he was invited to become the newspaper's editor. Smiles decided to abandon his career as a doctor and to become a full-time worker for the cause of political change. In the *Leeds Times* Smiles expressed his powerful dislike of the aristocracy and made attempts to unite working and middle-class reformers. Smiles also employed his newspaper in the campaign supporting factory legislation.

In May 1840 Smiles became Secretary to the Leeds Parliamentary Reform Association, an organization that believed in household suffrage (which would give the vote to the male head of every household), the secret ballot, equal representation, short parliaments, and the abolition of the property qualification for parliamentary candidates. In the 1840s Smiles became disillusioned with Chartism. Although Smiles still supported the six points of the Charter, he was worried by the growing influence of Fergus O'Connor, George Julian Harney, and the other advocates of Physical Force. Smiles argued, "Mere political reform will not cure the manifold evils which now afflict society." He stressed the importance of "individual reform" and promoted the idea of "self-help."

Smiles began to take a close interest in the ideas of Rober Owen. He contributed articles to Owens's journal, *The Union*. Smiles also helped the cooperative movement in Leeds. This included the Leeds Mutual Society and the Leeds Redemption Society.

In 1845 Samuel Smiles left the *Leeds Times* and became secretary to the Leeds and Thirsk Railway. After nine years with the Leeds and Thirsk Railway, he took up a similar post with the South-Eastern Railway.

In the 1850s Samuel Smiles completely abandoned his interest in parliamentary reform. He now argued that self-help provided the best route to success. His book *Self-Help*, which preached industry, thrift, and self-improvement, was published in 1859. Smiles also wrote a series of biographies of men who had achieved success through hard work. These included *George Stephenson* (1875), *Lives of the Engineers* (1861), and *Josiah Wedgwood* (1894). Samuel Smiles died in 1904.

Smiles's works have come to exemplify Victorian values and virtues for the modern reader. Smiles received some criticism in his own time from socialists because of his emphasis on individual achievement, but his popularity and acclaim reached a zenith in Victorian Britain. Among his many worthy quotations are:

A place for everything, and everything in its place.

An intense anticipation itself transforms possibility into reality; our desires being often but precursors of the things, which we are capable of performing.

Enthusiasm is the sustaining power of all great action.

He who never made a mistake, never made a discovery.

Hope is like the sun, which, as we journey toward it, casts the shadow of our burden behind us.

Hope is the companion of power, and mother of success; for whom so hopes strongly has within him the gift of miracles.

I'm as happy a man as any in the world, for the whole world seems to smile upon me!

It is a mistake to suppose that men succeed through success; they much oftener succeed through failures.

Precept, study, advice, and example could never have taught them as well as failure has done.

It is energy—the central element of which is will—that produces the miracle that is enthusiasm in all ages.

Everywhere it is what is called force of character and the sustaining power of all great action.

It will generally be found that men who are constantly lamenting their ill luck are only reaping the consequences of their own neglect, mismanagement, and improvidence, or want of application.

Knowledge conquered by labor becomes a possession—a property entirely our own.

Labor is still, and ever will be, the inevitable price set upon everything which is valuable.

Life will always be to a large extent what we ourselves make it.

Lost wealth may be replaced by industry, lost knowledge by study, lost health by temperance or medicine, but lost time is gone forever.

Man cannot aspire if he looked down; if he rises, he must look up.

Men must necessarily be the active agents of their own well-being and well-doing; they themselves must in the very nature of things be their own best helpers.

Men who are resolved to find a way for themselves will always find opportunities enough; and if they do not find them, they will make them.

Practical wisdom is only to be learned in the school of experience. Precepts and instruction are useful so far as they go, but without the discipline of real life, they remain of the nature of theory only.

Progress however, of the best kind, is comparatively slow. Great results cannot be achieved at once; and we must be satisfied to advance in life as we walk, step by step.

The apprenticeship of difficulty is one which the greatest of men have had to serve.

The battle of life is, in most cases, fought uphill; and to win it without a struggle were perhaps to win it without honor. If there were no difficulties there would be no success; if there were nothing to struggle for, there would be nothing to be achieved.

The duty of helping one's self in the highest sense involves the helping of one's neighbors.

The experience gathered from books, though often valuable, is but the nature of learning; whereas the experience gained from actual life is one of the natures of wisdom.

The reason why so little is done is generally because so little is attempted.

The shortest way to do many things is to do only one thing at once.

The spirit of self help is the root of all genuine growth in the individual.

The very greatest things—great thoughts, discoveries, inventions—have usually been nurtured in hardship, often pondered over in sorrow, and at length established with difficulty.

The wise man if he would live at peace with others, he will bear and forbear.

The work of many of the greatest men, inspired by duty, has been done amidst suffering and trial and difficulty. They have struggled against the tide, and reached the shore exhausted.

We learn wisdom from failure much more than from success. We often discover what will do, by finding out what will not do; and probably he who never made a mistake never made a discovery.

Wisdom and understanding can only become the possession of individual men by traveling the old road of observation, attention, perseverance, and industry.

Few people have argued so persuasively and consistently and with such passion and public effect about thrift, self-reliance, and duty as Samuel Smiles.

## JOHN MARKS TEMPLETON

Beginning a Wall Street career in 1937, John Templeton created some of the world's largest and most successful international investment funds. Termed "arguably the greatest global stock picker of the century" by *Money* magazine, he sold his various Templeton Funds in 1992 to the Franklin Group for $440 million. Becoming a naturalized British citizen living in Nassau, the Bahamas, Templeton was knighted Sir John by Queen Elizabeth II for his many accomplishments. One of those was creating the world's richest award, the $2 million Templeton Prize for Progress toward Research or Discoveries about Spiritual Realities, presented annually in London since 1972. And through the John Templeton Foundation, he gave away about $60 million a year—especially to projects, college courses, books, and essays on the benefits of cooperation between science and religion. The Foundation focuses on the really big questions, ones typically ignored by narrow specialists and fragmented studies.

Sir John M. Templeton, a student of benefits from free competition and disciplined work habits, wasn't the first wealthy investor to increase his giving to religion-related causes late in life. However, his progressive ideas on finance and faith made him a distinctive figure in both fields, perhaps something of an iconoclast. Not that the soft-spoken southerner worried about the distinction. "Rarely does a conservative become a hero of history," Templeton wrote in *The Humble Approach*, one of a dozen books he authored or edited. Rather, it is the far-reaching thinker who breaks out of the traditional mold... "one who, according to the accepted customs of his time, might be branded a heretic?"

Taking a less-traveled route in investing, Templeton sold advice on how to invest worldwide when Americans rarely considered foreign investment.

Standard stock-buying advice is "buy low, sell high." But Templeton took the strategy to an extreme—picking nations, industries, and companies hitting rock bottom "points of maximum pessimism," as he put it. When war began in Europe in 1939, he borrowed money to buy 100 shares in each of 104 companies selling at $1 a share or less, including some in bankruptcy. Only four turned out to be worthless, and he turned large profits on the others after holding each for an average of four years.

Templeton launched his flagship fund, Templeton Growth, Ltd., in 1954. It grew to total $455 million in 1999. Although he was a Presbyterian elder active in his denomination and on the boards of Princeton Theological Seminary and the American Bible Society, he espoused a "humble approach" to theology. Declaring that relatively little is known about God through scripture and present-day theologies, Templeton once predicted "scientific revelations may be a gold mine for revitalizing religion in the 21st century." His thrifty background and orientation are renowned. He lived and taught thrift as a core virtue.

The John Templeton Foundation donates to many entrepreneurs, trying various methods to increase our information about spiritual matters, especially through scientific research to supplement the wonderful ancient scriptures of all religions. For instance, the ambitious Forgiveness Project has funded more than $10 million in research investigating scientific bases for what religious traditions have instinctively taught concerning the salutary effect of forgiveness on offenders and victims alike.

John M. Templeton was born in 1912, in the small town of Winchester, Tennessee—a biographical fact bearing some irony, given that a dozen years later, in nearby Dayton, Tennessee, the famous Scopes "Monkey Trial" would unfold in a battle of evolution theory versus fundamentalist views of Creation. In contrast with that famously divisive episode, Templeton's foundation works on the premise that scientific principles of evolution and the idea of God as Creator are compatible and that seekers after truth should not quarrel but cooperate.

Forced to live thriftily by supporting himself while studying at Yale University during the Depression, Templeton graduated in 1934 as a top scholar in his class. He was named a Rhodes scholar to Balliol College at Oxford, from which he graduated with an M.A. degree in law. During a career that included directorships at banks, businesses, and insurance companies, Templeton maintained a long association with the Presbyterian Church (USA). For many years he was a trustee on the board of Princeton Theological Seminary, the largest Presbyterian seminary in the country, and he served as its chair for a dozen years. He also lent his business acumen to the Presbyterians' ministerial pension fund for more than three decades.

Templeton was known for starting his mutual funds' annual meetings with a prayer. He explained that the devotional words were not pleas for financial gain in the mundane world but meditations to calm and clear the minds of managers and stockholders. Templeton often told interviewers that "competitive business," in his view, matched in many ways the compassionate aims of religious bodies. "For one thing, it enriched the poor more that any other system humanity ever has had," he told *Insight* magazine. "Competitive business has reduced costs, has increased variety, and has improved quality." And if a business is not ethical, he added, "it will fail, perhaps not right away, but eventually."

Typical of Templeton's wide-lens view of spirituality and ethics, the dedicated Presbyterian admitted to additional influence from the New Thought movements of Christian Science, Unity, and Religious Science. Those metaphysical churches espouse a nonliteral view of heaven and hell and suggest a shared divinity between God and humanity. "We realize that our own divinity arises from something more that merely being God's children or being made in his image," Templeton wrote. Sir John did not claim credentials as a theologian as much as someone with enough money to stir new research pursuing further "knowledge and love of God."

Sir John M. Templeton was more than a famous but humble investor and one of the founders of mutual funds. In his generous philanthropic life he came to a few key conclusions, one of them revolving around the importance of thrift and its responsible cousin, generosity. Life in many ways embodies the marriage of thrift and charity. Studying the teachings of the laws of the spirit, he suggested, benefits humanity in even greater measure than does, for example, studying the laws of chemistry. He cited Matthew Arnold, who thought that the decreasing influence of the

Bible that commenced in the nineteenth century could be reversed if the ideals, hopes, and laws expressed in the poetic and allegorical language of the scriptures could be explained experimentally. In that sense dogmatic theology could be replaced by empirical theology and the nexus between science and religion made more evident. If everyday people could understand religious principles in their own language rather than in ancient metaphors, they might take them more seriously. Believing, for instance, that self-reliance depends on making decisions for oneself rather than depending on others would build a stronger person and society. Furthermore, according to Templeton, concentrating the mind on positive and productive things would lead to greater material success and greater wealth, which themselves flow from spiritual growth and progress.

Templeton is remembered foremost for reminding typically narcissistic moderns that "you have something they never had." To quote Sir John, "I have often been asked about the psyche and role of high-net worth individuals and how they could connect with leading scholars and others who could benefit from their partnership and acumen. Such partnering is an essential part of philanthropy and a vital source for both the grantee and grantor."

Despite all his wealth, organization, and power, Templeton was most interested in the power of partnering. *"Wishing me with him, partner of his fortune,"* as Shakespeare put it in *Two Gentleman of Verona*, bearing witness to the fact that the idea of partners has indeed been around for a very long time. Templeton constantly sought to regenerate it in both his style of doing business as an investor in distant markets and later as funder and philanthropist of so many invigorating projects concerning the nexus of science and religion.

He thought that, until a few years ago, large, integrated organizations were the undisputed king of the world, in private, public, and social sectors of the economy. Now that crown is contested by *groups* of organizations working in concert. The intensity of competition has not abated, but the nature of rivalry has changed. *Cooperation* is ceasing to be the polar opposite of competition and is instead one of the preferred instruments of engagement in today's world. Could this too be the evolution of philanthropic efforts?

First, the *good news*: there is a strategy that can bring 25 percent greater value than that of all others. And now the *bad news*: too many organizations do not try or can't make the strategy work. The strategy Templeton favored is, of course, partnering. Partnering is the ability to create value through skillful management of portfolios of business relationships as an important source of competitive advantage. It has now become essential in this new millennium. He wanted to challenge philanthropists and wealthy people and families around the globe to consider the benefit of partnering with others of like mind to achieve a greater good.

For Templeton, the trend toward more partnering reflected not a sudden outbreak of excitement but a belief that in a fast-changing and ever more complex, risky environment, organizations must look beyond their own boundaries and seek to create *win-win* relationships with others that provide complementary capabilities. As he found in his years on Wall Street, mutuality in every sense distributes both risks and rewards.

Sir John said in one of his many books, "At my advanced age, I am most optimistic about an outlook on philanthropy that is rooted in vision, willing to innovate, and that takes collaboration seriously. This is the challenge of this century: to increase our knowledge 100 fold. To do so we must strive together challenging wealth to take a seat at the table with wisdom."

In adopting a host of partnering strategies, philanthropic organizations acknowledge that, in practice if not in theory, the need for control can be less pressing than the need to create or extend networks of business and social relationships in order to get things done. "Going it alone" is less and less an option, so smart organizations feel they must collaborate.

For Templeton the critical strategic drivers that frame and inform the decision to partner were many, ranging from common vision to shared strategy, from value chain optimization to standard setting, and from technology to increased effectiveness. None may be more significant in this Internet era than Metcalfe's *Law of Networks,* which tells us that the value of a network varies according to the square of its size, giving first movers a huge advantage.

What can improve partnerships in venture philanthropy? Experience demonstrates that time spent on the compatibility of values, common visions, cooperative management styles, knowledge sharing, and the all-important building of trust is time well spent. In the end, partnerships work *only* to the degree that partners deeply trust one another. For the indefinite future, partnering is not going away, according to Templeton. It is simply one way to do *more* with *less*, even to achieve breakthroughs not hitherto possible. In the world of philanthropy, the incentives of the marketplace are not always fully operative; therefore philanthropists must experiment more and must always seek to leverage their limited funds and distinct capabilities. They need to partner with scholars, researchers, and other like charitable organizations to *maximize* their overall effect. In a strict sense, Templeton's view of partnership and collaboration was very much part and parcel of his Scottish heritage. He saw thrift as a core virtue that needed to be rediscovered, even reinvented.

Philanthropies have in the past been at best too wary and watchful. More of them need to share research, due diligence, best practices, and even the costs of defined projects. All kinds of alliances and joint ventures are possible for those willing to treat their philanthropy more like venture capital. Just think of the combination of effort and the likely benefits. Here is a positive, bold, new vision for a robust, extremely entrepreneurial venturing kind of philanthropy that is willing and able to partner so as to make possible new things, new cures, more innovations and scientific research and advancement in spiritual information to the benefit of persons everywhere and for decades and centuries to come.

Sir John said, "As true partners, we need to bring together private philanthropists, foundation leaders, and pioneering researchers to explore the role that innovation can play in shaping the strategy, practices, and impact of philanthropy across the entire spectrum of giving. Only then will we witness acceleration in philanthropic progress." Thrift, hard work, and cooperative partnering were a sort of trinity for Templeton, and they made him one of the most generous people to inhabit the earth.

These three heroes of virtue can teach us a great deal of wisdom about wealth, savings, and most particularly the nature and virtue of thrift. If only we would take the time to benefit from their acumen and sage experience. In so doing we would rediscover a lost virtue.

# INDEX